A GUIDE TO
Reading the Runes

Harness the wisdom and power of the ancient Norse symbols

Laura Daligan

CICO BOOKS

FOR ODIN AND FOR STAR.

Published in 2025 by CICO Books
An imprint of Ryland Peters & Small Ltd
20–21 Jockey's Fields   1452 Davis Bugg Road
London WC1R 4BW   Warrenton, NC 27589
www.rylandpeters.com
Email: euregulations@rylandpeters.com

10 9 8 7 6 5 4 3 2 1

Text © Laura Daligan 2025
Design and illustration © CICO Books 2025
Additional illustrations (backgrounds): Adobe Stock/ANEK

The author's moral rights have been asserted. All rights reserved. No part of this publication may be reproduced, stored in a retrieval system, or transmitted in any form or by any means, electronic, mechanical, photocopying, or otherwise, without the prior permission of the publisher.

A CIP record for this book is available from the British Library.
US Library of Congress CIP data has been applied for.

ISBN: 978 1 80065 453 2

Printed in China

Illustrator: Emma Taylor
Illustrator (borders, p40, p62): Victoria Fomina
Commissioning editor: Kristine Pidkameny
Editor: Imogen Valler-Miles
Senior designer: Emily Breen
Art director: Sally Powell
Creative director: Leslie Harrington
Production manager: Gordana Simakovic
Head of production: Patricia Harrington
Publishing manager: Carmel Edmonds

The authorised representative in the EEA is
Authorised Rep Compliance Ltd.,
Ground Floor, 71 Lower Baggot Street,
Dublin, D01 P593, Ireland
www.arccompliance.com

Safety note: Neither the author nor the publisher can be held responsible for any claim arising out of the general information and practices provided in this book. Please note that while the use of essential oils, incense, and particular practices refer to healing benefits, they are not intended to replace diagnosis of illness or ailments, or healing or medicine. Always consult your doctor or other health professional in the case of illness. Essential oils are very powerful and potentially toxic if used too liberally. Please follow the advice given on the label and never use the oils neat on bare skin, or if pregnant. The safe and proper use of candles is the sole responsibility of the person using them. Do not leave a burning candle unattended. Never burn a candle on or near anything that might catch fire. Keep candles out of the reach of children and pets.

A GUIDE TO Reading the Runes

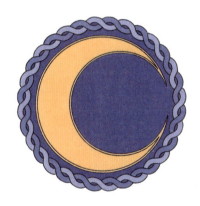

Contents

An invitation... 6

CHAPTER 1
The history of the runes 8

CHAPTER 2
Meeting the runes 20

CHAPTER 3
Divination with the runes 94

CHAPTER 4
The runic path 114

Conclusion 139

Glossary 140

Bibliography and resources 141

Index 142

Acknowledgments 144

An invitation...

Welcome to this journey with the runes. Whether you are new to this path, or are seeking to deepen your knowledge, I hope you will find magic and inspiration within these pages.

This book has grown from a lifelong love of magic, mythology, divination, and history. I first discovered the runes around twenty-five years ago, but for some years they remained on the periphery of my magical life. I felt them, and the Norse gods, calling, but it wasn't until a few years later that I became fully immersed in all things runic. In the end, I heeded the call of the gods and dived in headfirst. I studied the magical, healing, and shamanic aspects of the runes, and also completed a master's degree in Viking Studies, specializing in the myth and magic of the Viking Age.

    Learning the runes is a wild, wonderful, and healing journey, which can be both enjoyable and transformational. Throughout this book, you will learn the stories, magic, and meanings of each rune, and discover powerful ways of working with them in the modern world. Although I examine a multitude of myths and lore from the pre-Christian North, this is not an academic study of the runic alphabet, but an invitation to meet and journey with the runes. If you feel at all intimidated by the runes, or find them hard to access, please do not worry or be put off. Be patient with yourself, and the runes will share their wisdom with you in time.

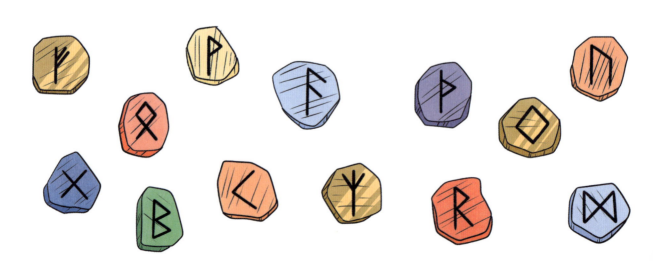

As you gain more confidence with the Elder Futhark runic alphabet (page 11), I invite you to read as broadly as you can and discover your own nuanced meanings. Research the source texts, such as the Eddas and the rune poems (page 12), and experiment with the exercises and practices within this book. A glossary of terms that you may be unfamiliar with is provided on page 140. You can learn the basic art of reading the runes in a fairly short amount of time, but the initiatory journey they can lead us on can last a lifetime.

Sometimes, when I look at the runes, they open doorways of deep understanding, and at other times, all I see are simple engravings of vertical, horizontal, and diagonal lines! Their raw simplicity is an invitation to remember something embedded deep within, and so I look, I feel, and I listen…

From this space, they begin to share the wisdom that is hidden within their angular forms. I hear their voices reverberating deep in the earth and spiraling up to the heavens. I listen as their songs weave meaning into the threads of my life, and I journey with them through the leaves of Yggdrasil. My world expands through ice, rock, and fire, as stars wheel and gods spread their wings. Beneath mighty roots, three women carve songs of fate as silver waters softly ripple upon tides of memory.

I look again, and those ancient, simple lines are shining.

CHAPTER

The history of the runes

The name "rune" has several meanings, including "secret," "hidden," "poem," and "letter." This mix of mundane and arcane meanings reflects the multifaceted ways that the runes can be understood and used. Although the runes form a practical writing system, the letters can also be seen as symbols representing divine powers and cosmological energies.

The runes are not static letters but dynamic energies, flowing along the threads of fate…

The origin of the runes

Runes are a series of angular symbols that formed the writing system of the Germanic peoples of northern Europe. Typically, runes were carved into wood, stone, metal, and bone.

THE RUNIC ALPHABETS

The Elder Futhark is the oldest known form of runic alphabet and is comprised of twenty-four runes. Its origin is a contentious subject. However, current evidence suggests that it was in use from approximately 50 CE to 700 CE. The name "Futhark" or "Fuþark" comes from the first six letters of the alphabet (Fehu, Uruz, Thurisaz, Ansuz, Raidho, and Kenaz) with "þ" representing the "th" sound. Shortly after 700 CE, a radically simplified and modified runic alphabet came into use in Scandinavia, called the Younger Futhark, which consisted of sixteen runes, and by the tenth century it had completely replaced the Elder Futhark.

The fullness of the Elder Futhark was not only preserved in the Anglo-Saxon runic alphabet but expanded upon. The Anglo-Saxon, or Anglo-Frisian, Futhark contains at least twenty-eight runes, and is believed to have been in use from approximately 400 CE to 1300 CE. In his book *The Hobbit*, J.R.R. Tolkien used the Anglo-Saxon runes to depict the dwarves' writing, which can be seen on Thrór's map, describing the way into the lonely mountain.

Alphabets are magical by nature: they inform and construct how we relate to the world and to each other. They create communion and add power and meaning to our lives. It is not hard to believe that the very symbols that could name the gods could also contain the powers to invoke them. Although all the runic alphabets can be used for divination and magical purposes, it is the oldest, the Elder Futhark, which is most commonly worked with and is the focus of this book.

THE ELDER FUTHARK

The twenty-four runes of the Elder Futhark can be divided into three groups of eight, known as an Ætt, which is an Old Norse term for a clan or family. Each Ætt expresses its own fundamental meanings that permeate through the rune row. We will explore these in detail in Chapter 2.

THE FIRST ÆTT

Fehu   Uruz   Thurisaz   Ansuz   Raidho   Kenaz   Gebo   Wunjo

THE SECOND ÆTT

Hagalaz   Nauthiz   Isa   Jera   Eihwaz   Perthro   Algiz   Sowilo

THE THIRD ÆTT

Teiwaz   Berkano   Ehwaz   Mannaz   Laguz   Inguz   Othala   Dagaz

RUNIC INSCRIPTIONS

In ancient times, specific runes were inscribed onto objects or intoned to invoke gods, to ask for protection or healing, and to ensure victory. Inscriptions containing magical incantations and invocations have been discovered, but they are few and far between. For the most part, runic inscriptions contained practical information and were found on memorial stones or used for declaring ownership of objects or places. Although many modern pagans like to consider runic scripts as a strictly pagan endeavor, a large number of inscriptions are from Christian sources or carved by Christians.

THE RUNE POEMS AND EDDAS

Much of our knowledge of the runes comes from the three rune poems: the Old Norse rune poem, the Anglo-Saxon rune poem, and the Old Icelandic rune poem. Not all of the runes feature in each poem, but each rune has at least one poem to its name. The Norse and Icelandic poems are based on the Younger Futhark, while the Anglo-Saxon poem focuses on the Anglo-Saxon Futhark. If there was ever a poem for the Elder Futhark, it is no longer known.

It is thought that the Anglo-Saxon rune poem was composed in the eighth or ninth century CE and was recorded circa the tenth century. The Old Norse rune poem is recorded in a seventeenth-century copy of a thirteenth-century manuscript, and the Old Icelandic rune poem was correlated from different manuscripts dating from the fifteenth century. The poems contain tantalizing glimpses into Viking Age, Anglo-Saxon, and medieval life, with the verses often containing riddles and referencing kennings (see page 140) and folklore. Some scholars believe the poems to be simple writing exercises, whereas others, myself included, believe that the poems' rich symbolism hints at the runes' deeper meanings.

The main sources for comprehending Old Norse mythology and cosmology are the *Poetic Edda* and *Snorri's Edda*, also called the *Prose Edda*. The *Poetic Edda* was compiled in Iceland in the late thirteenth century, and comprises several mythological poems, including the *Völuspá* and *Hávamál*. The manuscript was either lost or hidden for 400 years and was rediscovered by a bishop in 1642. *Snorri's Edda* was written by the Icelandic politician, historian, and poet, Snorri Sturluson, between 1220 and 1225. It narrates the origins of the worlds, and the creation and adventures of the gods, elves, dwarves, and giants, through to the inescapable, cataclysmic events of Ragnarök. *Snorri's Edda* is made up of four parts, including *Gylfaginning* and *Skáldskaparmál*.

I refer to and discuss the different source texts throughout this book, and they are included in the bibliography (page 141) if you would like to study them in more detail.

12 THE HISTORY OF THE RUNES

Old Norse cosmology

If we wish to understand the mysteries of the runes, we need to place them within the context of the Old Norse worldview. Runes are a living part of the web of existence, and for people of the pre-Christian North, this web was vast, complex, elemental, and inhabited by many magical and powerful beings...

THE NORSE CREATION MYTH

In the beginning, there was nothing, except the yawning void of Ginnungagap. On one side of the void emerged a dark world of mist and ice called Niflheimr, and on the other side, a world of fire was forged called Múspellsheimr. Over time, the sparks of fire from Múspellsheimr flew out and began to melt the ice of Niflheimr. This caused vast swirling clouds of vapor and mist to appear in the center of Ginnungagap. As fire and ice mixed, rivers began to flow and poured into the heart of the void.

From this cauldron of chaos and potential emerged the first being, the giant Ymir. The primal cosmic cow, Auðumbla, followed soon after, feeding Ymir with her milk. Auðumbla wandered the vast, misty realms, nourishing herself by licking blocks of salty ice. As she licked, the ice began to melt and she saw that beings were frozen within it. She licked them until they were free, and this was the birth of the first gods.

The first god was called Buri and he had a son, named Burr. With the giantess Bestla, Burr fathered three children, named Odin, Hœnir, and Lóðurr. The sons of Burr decided to murder Ymir, and from this cosmic violence, the world was made. Ymir's blood is the sea and lakes, his bones are mountains, and his skull became the heavens, which is held in place by four dwarves who represent the four cardinal directions. Embers of fire from Múspellsheimr became the sun, moon, and stars.

While walking by the sea, Odin, Hœnir, and Lóðurr found two logs of driftwood upon the shore. The three gods could see shapes in the wood and they began to carve them. From these pieces of wood, the first humans were made and their names were Ask (meaning "ash tree") and Embla (perhaps meaning "elm" or "vine"). They went on to dwell in Miðgarðr, the world of humanity.

Numerous other worlds were also created and, although we can't be sure how many there are, we do know of the existence of nine, including ours.

THE NINE WORLDS

1. **Asgard (Old Norse: Ásgarðr)** A mountainous place with rich valleys and fields, and home to the Æsir gods (the gods of civilization). Each god and goddess has their own magnificent hall. Interestingly, the gods are also said to have temples and altars where they worship, but we do not know who, or what, they worship.

2. **Midgard (Old Norse: Miðgarðr)** This is the middle dwelling and our home, the world of humanity! Midgard is meant to be similar to Asgard and situated close to it. The rainbow bridge Bifröst links these two worlds, so when we see a rainbow, we know that the Æsir gods are present. Around the circumference of Midgard is a primeval ocean and in those waters dwells Jörmungandr, the Midgard serpent.

3. **Vanaheim (Old Norse: Vanaheimr)** This is the home of the Vanir tribe of gods, who are the gods of the land. The two tribes of gods were locked in a long war, which ended only with an exchange of hostages. The Vanir god Njörðr and his twins Freyja and Freyr went to live with the Æsir and became intrinsic parts of the mythologies.

4. **Jötunheim (Old Norse: Jötunheimr)** The home of the *jötnar* (giants), Jötunheim is a place of primal power. It is a vast and varied place, filled with wild dangers, but it is also a world of adventure, magic, and creativity. The giants can represent chaos and the sovereignty of the land. They appear often in the sagas and are usually at odds with the gods. Although Thor and his hammer destroy countless giants, both Odin and Thor are descended from giants.

5. **Helheim, also known as Hel (Old Norse: Helheimr)** One of the worlds of the dead, Hel is a vast underworld realm, ruled over by Queen Hel, the goddess of the dead. Hel was not a place of punishment, but rather a place of rest, where most people were expected to go if they died of illness or old age. Beneath Hel is a place called Niflhel, meaning "misty Hel," which holds the lowest levels of the underworld and digs deep into the cold, dark earth.

6. **Alfheim and Svartalfheim (Old Norse: Álfheimr and Svartálfheimr)** Alfheim is the home of the light elves, who are said to be shining and more beautiful than the sun. Svartalheim is the realm of the dark elves, and is described as being underground and can perhaps be linked with the fertility of the earth. Dark elves are sometimes considered to be identical to dwarves. There are various types of elves and, in some cases, the Vanir and the elves are the same beings. Freyr was gifted Alfheim when he gained his first tooth. Everyday people who were close to the land may have connected with elves more than the gods.

7. **Nidavellir (Old Norse: Niðavellir)** This is the home of the dwarves, who are viewed as shorter than the gods and less attractive. They are thought to live in the earth and are greatly skilled with crafts and metalwork. The dwarves made many magical treasures for the gods including: Freyja's necklace, Brísingamen; Thor's hammer, Mjölnir; and Freyr's ship, Skíðblaðnir.
8. **Niflheim (Old Norse: Niflheimr)** This is the primal place of ice and mists, and home to ancient ice giants. In some of the source texts, Niflheim is used interchangeably with Hel and Niflhel.
9. **Muspelheim (Old Norse: Múspellsheimr)** The primal place of fire, Muspelheim is home to the fire giants. It is guarded by the fire giant Surtr and his flaming sword.

YGGDRASIL

The center of all of these worlds is Yggdrasil, also known as the world tree, or the tree of life. Yggdrasil's vast roots and branches reach out across all of existence, connecting all life. It is generally considered to be a great ash tree but is sometimes connected with the evergreen yew tree. Yggdrasil means "Odin's Steed," referencing the sacrifice that Odin made by hanging from the tree (page 16).

Three wells lie nestled beneath the roots of Yggdrasil. Their names are Urðarbrunnr, Mímisbrunnr, and Hvergelmir. Each well nourishes the world tree and represents different aspects of consciousness. Urðarbrunnr is the well of fate and memory and is tended by the Norns. Mímisbrunnr belongs to the wise god Mímir and is the well of wisdom and intelligence. Hvergelmir, meaning "bubbling cauldron," lies at the heart of Niflheim, and from its primal waters spring all the rivers of the world.

Journeying with Odin

In Old Norse mythology, it is Odin—the All-Father of the Æsir gods—who not only discovered the runes but also shared them with mankind. Odin is considered to be the chief of the gods and is a powerful and complex deity. We will meet him several times throughout this book, as he takes a special interest in those who wish to study the magic of the runes.

Odin is a sorcerer and a shape-shifter and can magically transform into the shape of an animal, such as a snake, a fish, or an eagle. He has a deep affinity with ravens, and one of his many names is Hrafnaguð, meaning Raven-God. His own ravens, Huginn (meaning "thought") and Muninn (meaning "memory"), carry aspects of his mind and soul across the nine worlds of Old Norse cosmology. Although he has many roles, titles, and names, Odin's primary concern is his quest for wisdom. Odin is known to journey between the different worlds on his quest for knowledge. The poem *Hávamál*, meaning "Sayings of the High One," is part of the *Poetic Edda* and it describes the lengths he will go to in order to acquire sacred knowledge. It recounts how Odin sacrificed himself by hanging from Yggdrasil for nine days, stabbed with his own spear, in order to create an initiatory experience that led to his discovery of the runes. You do not need to work with Odin in order to work with the runes. However, it is a good idea to meet him before you begin, because his help and support will likely be a great blessing upon your journey.

The pathworking meditation on pages 18–19 has been created to guide you on a sacred journey to meet Odin. You may wish to record yourself speaking through this meditation, so that you can relax and listen to the recording any time you wish to connect with the All-Father. While recording, remember to speak slowly and allow yourself the space to explore the magical landscape of this journey. If you are learning the runes with a friend, it might be helpful to take turns, reading the journey for each other.

Whether you are new to the runes or are deepening your connection, this meditation blesses and honors your runic pathway. With this in mind, you may like to light a candle or take a moment to consider what drew you to this path in the first place. What would you like to learn from Odin? There are no right or wrong answers; this is simply an opportunity to focus on your experiences, hopes, and intentions.

If possible, journal your experience as soon as you finish the meditation. Just as dreams can vanish from our minds upon waking, so can the powerful details of a pathworking meditation when we return to our daily routine and habits. If for any reason you feel ungrounded or wobbly after the meditation, stamp your feet on the ground a few times, move your body, shake out your arms and legs, and have a little something to eat or drink.

MEDITATION: MEETING ODIN

1. When you are ready, sit in a comfortable place where you won't be disturbed. Begin by taking some deep breaths, inhaling through your nose and exhaling through your mouth. Visualize a silver light flowing through your body on your in-breath, and release any worries or intruding thoughts on your out-breath, releasing with a big sigh. In your mind's eye, see those thoughts leaving your body like gray smoke, which transforms on the air into light and returns to source. Repeat this process a few more times.

2. With your eyes closed, visualize or sense the room around you. Picture the furniture, the walls, and the floor as if your eyes were open. As you do this, you begin to see a silver and white mist flowing in from the corners of the room. It flows around you, from one space to another. It fills the room until all you see is the mist.

3. The mist begins to clear and you find yourself walking along a moonlit path. The vastness of the heavens stretches out above you as you look in wonder at the myriad stars wheeling above. The moon lights your way clearly and you become aware that the path is leading you toward the roots of an enormous tree. This is Yggdrasil, the tree of life. Its branches reach up high into the starlit night, so high that you cannot see where they end.

4. Suddenly, you hear the call of ravens, and notice that there are two ravens flying above you, guiding you toward the great tree. As you approach the vast roots, the ravens perch on the lower branches, looking at you curiously as they preen their feathers. Between two of the roots is a deep well. The water in the well appears to faintly glow silver and white under the moonlight. You feel in your bones that this is a sacred well, and keep a respectful distance, but the soft sound of water and the dancing leaves above creates a music that stirs something deep within you.

5. You are so absorbed in the wonder of this place that it takes you a moment to realize that you are not alone. A man stands in front of the tree. You didn't see or hear him approaching and wonder if perhaps he has always been there. The man is tall and clad in gray and blue. He wears a rimmed hat that covers one of his eyes while his other eye gleams at you like star fire. This is the god Odin, and he has come to meet you at the beginning of your journey.

6. As you introduce yourself, he looks up and says that his ravens alerted him to your arrival. He steps closer toward you and asks why you have journeyed here. In your own time, answer him honestly. Your answer appears to please him, and he turns toward Yggdrasil, and places one hand upon the bark. As he does so, streams of golden light run up and down the tree, and as you look closely, you notice that all the runes are contained within them.

7. Odin looks directly into your eyes, and it feels like he is staring into the heart of you. He turns once more to the tree and reaches into the golden stream, picking out a rune and placing it into your open hands, saying, "This rune opens the gateways for the beginning of your journey." You study the rune as it manifests in physical form in your hands. What color is it? What material is it? Do you recognize the symbol? You look up to thank the All-Father, and realize that he is nowhere to be seen. There is nothing remaining of his presence except the rune in your hand, and a single raven's feather floating to the ground in front of you.

8. The golden light fades from the tree and you know that it is time for you to return home. You step back onto the moonlit path and slowly walk away from the tree, all the while contemplating your experience with Odin and the rune in your hand. As you walk, you become aware of that familiar silver-and-white mist appearing from the corners of your vision. It flows all around you, until the tree and the path disappear and all you can see is the mist. When the mist begins to clear again, you find yourself safely back in your home, your space—grounded and ready to continue your day.

The rune that Odin chose for you will be an important and personal one for you at the start of your runic journey. Don't worry if you don't recognize the symbol yet—sit with it for a few minutes, draw its shape, and journal your impressions of it. Remember, there are no wrong answers, so allow your own thoughts about the rune to flow. When you are ready, turn to the pages about your rune in Chapter 2 and consider how these meanings and correspondences relate to you and your path at this time.

JOURNEYING WITH ODIN 19

CHAPTER  2

Meeting the runes

Throughout this chapter, we will meet the twenty-four runes of the Elder Futhark alphabet. Each rune embodies and expresses a wealth of energies, stories, correspondences, and interpretations. There are no limits to how you can work with the runes; it is a lifelong journey of soulful discoveries.

Introducing the runes

The runes of the Elder Futhark are split into three rows of eight, called Ætts. Each Ætt expresses intrinsic meanings that permeate through the row.

The three Ætts are journeys, leading us through the fundamental experiences of life, death, and rebirth. From the primal powers of creation to the external and internal forces that impact our daily lives, the Ætts are guides and challengers that ultimately support the forging of our own unique paths. Each Ætt is associated with a specific deity, and the runes within an Ætt are connected with one another through shared themes and concepts.

Throughout this chapter, we will explore each of the twenty-four runes in turn, delving into their complex and multifaceted meanings and symbolism. Some rune sets include a twenty-fifth rune, known as the blank rune. I don't work with this rune, but you can find information about it on page 93, in case you do wish to include it in your rune work.

You are invited to work with the runes in a variety of ways. You could meditate on the rune, intone and chant it, draw it, and connect with its many correspondences. The correspondences I have listed include the rune's associated deities, elements, colors, animals, trees, plants, oils, and crystals and minerals (which also encompasses rocks, gems, and metals). Also included are keywords, as well as the rune's corresponding letter (or sound) from the modern Latin alphabet.

We will explore the historical background and symbolic meaning of each rune and I also weave in relevant stories from the rune poems, Eddas, and sagas (page 12) throughout. Finally, I share suggestions for how you can experience each rune in your day-to-day life, including their meanings in divination. The runes contain a wealth of knowledge and wisdom but, ultimately, their meanings are open to interpretation, and I encourage you to venture on your own personal journey of runic exploration.

You are invited to conduct your own research and select which meanings and stories resonate with you. For each rune, I have shared a brief poem inspired by the runes' energies, but I encourage you to contribute to the fabric of rune wisdom by recording and creating your own runic reflections.

Once we have met and connected with the runes, in chapters 3 and 4, we will explore runic divination in detail, as well as a multitude of other ways you can go deeper with your runic path.

THE FIRST ÆTT—FREYJA AND FREYR'S ÆTT (PAGE 24)

| Fehu | Uruz | Thurisaz | Ansuz | Raidho | Kenaz | Gebo | Wunjo |
| (page 26) | (page 28) | (page 31) | (page 34) | (page 36) | (page 39) | (page 42) | (page 44) |

THE SECOND ÆTT—HEIMDALL'S ÆTT (PAGE 46)

| Hagalaz | Nauthiz | Isa | Jera | Eihwaz | Perthro | Algiz | Sowilo |
| (page 48) | (page 51) | (page 53) | (page 56) | (page 59) | (page 61) | (page 64) | (page 67) |

THE THIRD ÆTT—TÝR'S ÆTT (PAGE 70)

| Teiwaz | Berkano | Ehwaz | Mannaz | Laguz | Inguz | Othala | Dagaz |
| (page 72) | (page 74) | (page 77) | (page 80) | (page 82) | (page 85) | (page 88) | (page 91) |

INTRODUCING THE RUNES 23

THE FIRST ÆTT

Freyja and Freyr's Ætt

The first Ætt belongs to the divine twins Freyja and Freyr. Although this rune family is sometimes referred to as solely Freyja's Ætt, I prefer the fertility, balance, and harmony suggested by the pairing.

Freyja and Freyr (meaning "Lady" and "Lord") are two of the most renowned deities of the Germanic world, and are the foremost deities of the Vanir tribe of gods. The Vanir are primarily seen as fertility gods, connected with the land, the weather, agriculture, and seafaring. They were at war with the Æsir gods for a long and painful time. To ensure peace between the tribes, each tribe sent hostages to live with the other tribe. Freyja and Freyr were the Vanir gods who went to live with the Æsir.

Freyja is a goddess of fertility, love, magic, and prophecy. It was, in fact, Freyja who taught Odin the Norse practice of sorcery known as *seiðr*. Freyja's powers are present in the wealth of the land and within the realms of the dead. After battles, she would choose half of the slain warriors to dwell in her realm of Fólkvangr (meaning "field" or "meadow of the people"), while the other half went to reside in Odin's hall, Valhalla. Freyja has a strong connection with the animal kingdom and can shape-shift into falcon form with the use of her feathered cloak, called a *válshamr*.

Freyr is the most popular Vanir god, and has several place-names attributed to him across Norway and Sweden, including Freyshof ("Freyr's temple"), Freyssteinn ("Freyr's stone"), and Fröslunda ("Freyr's grove"). He is a god of agriculture and fertility, and also of sacred kingship. Freyr married the giantess Gerðr after he sent his servant, Skírnir, on a quest to woo her for him. Skírnir agreed, but only on the condition that he could take Freyr's magical sword with him. Even without his sword, Freyr was still able to defeat the giant Beli using only an antler for a weapon.

Freyja and Freyr's Ætt represents the primal elements of creation and destruction. This Ætt embodies the life cycle and conveys the fundamental qualities that we need for a healthy and balanced life.

Rising sap and greening spring
The urge to create, the spark to begin

Fehu (fay-oo)

While its literal meaning is "cattle," Fehu is the rune of pure life force, luck, power, and movement.

Keywords: Abundance, Wealth, Cattle, Vitality, Sensuality, Fertility
Letter: F
Deities: Freyja, Freyr, the Vanir
Elements: Fire, Earth
Colors: Gold, Red, Green
Animals: Cattle, Cat, Dragon, Pig, Snake, Wolf
Tree: Elder
Oil: Cinnamon
Crystals & Minerals: Gold, Amber, Carnelian

The origin of the name The Old Norse name for Fehu is "Fe," which is still used today in our word for payments, "fee." The Old Norse rune poem speaks of the problems that money and hoarded wealth can bring, conjuring up fearful images of wolves waiting in the dark ready to attack. Although the Anglo-Saxon rune poem focuses on the comforts of abundance, it also advises that wealth should be shared. Gift-giving and displays of generosity were important aspects of Viking Age society. In times when there were few social infrastructures in place, the sharing of wealth created and reinforced important bonds of kinship and support.

The shape of Fehu Fehu can be interpreted as depicting the horns of a cow, and historically the rune represented cattle. For our ancestors, cattle would have signified sustenance, power, and mobile wealth. One cow in particular played an integral role within the mythologies. She is the primal cow named Auðumbla, who nourished the first beings with her milk, and can be seen as an ancient mother goddess. She created the first god by licking stones of salty ice; as the ice diminished, a man was slowly revealed. His name was Buri, and he came to be the grandfather of Odin. Just as Auðumbla brought life, warmth, and nourishment to the world, so Fehu inspires these qualities within us.

Freyja's rune Fehu is a feminine force and is traditionally known as Freyja's rune. Freyja is a goddess who presides over matters of love, magic, sensuality, fertility, and abundance, all of which are intrinsically linked with Fehu's energies.

26 MEETING THE RUNES

Luck spirits In the Old Norse worldview, in order to attract success and abundance, we would need to have a positive relationship with our *hamingja*, which is a personified spirit of luck. Unless we are extremely unlucky, we each have a *hamingja*, and our relationship with it is nurtured by our own positive actions. However, it is possible that our luck spirits may tire of our behavior and decide to desert us, which actually happens several times in the sagas. This departure of the *hamingja* is the origin of the phrase, "a person's luck has run out on them."

FEHU IN PRACTICE

We can feel Fehu in our bodies as a fresh and bright current of life force. Fehu relates to the blood pumping through our veins and the fiery spark of desire. It is a rune of fulfillment and warmth. We can work with Fehu to boost self-confidence and to invoke vitality when we are feeling exhausted or low. As a rune connected with Freyja and sensuality, Fehu reminds us to not only be present in our bodies, but to *enjoy* our bodies.

We can feel Fehu in the land as the rising sap and the magic of photosynthesis. Fehu is present in the wild places, in the unfurling trees, and basking in the warming sun. Spending time in nature's green spaces increases the flow of Fehu within our lives. One thing we must remember is that this rune thrives on flow and movement. We cannot hold on to it too tightly, nor hide our gold away in treasure chests. The warnings against hoarding wealth are of equal importance to us today as they were in the Viking Age.

Chanting Fehu enhances the life force in our own body and can also be used to charge magical items with the energy of the rune.

Divination meanings

- Fehu signifies a time of potential abundance and increased wealth.
- It can also indicate health and vitality returning.
- Creative projects and all areas of fertility are blessed by Fehu.
- Fehu can mark the beginning of a new venture and inspires confidence and success.
- This rune warns against greed, hoarding, stagnation, and exploitation.

Before plague pits rose
The wild aurochs roamed
And your song was the river

Uruz (oo-rooz)

Building upon the elemental vitality sparked by Fehu, Uruz is the manifestation of courage, strength, and physical vigor. It is the will to channel nature's wildness and is a rune of formation.

Keywords: Strength, Endurance, Courage, Healing, Aurochs
Letter: U
Deities: Thor, Jord, Buri, Urðr
Elements: Earth, Water
Colors: Orange, Red, Brown, Green
Animals: Aurochs, Wild Cattle, Reindeer
Tree: Birch
Oil: Cypress
Crystals & Minerals: Garnet, Amber, Rocks

Ancient aurochs The literal meaning of Uruz is "aurochs," a huge and now extinct type of wild cattle. The aurochs is the much larger, wild ancestor of all modern cattle, which would have roamed and shaped the landscape for hundreds of thousands of years. Aurochs have been depicted in cave paintings from as far back as the Paleolithic period. The shape of Uruz can be seen as the aurochs' distinctive horns, or as the "hump" of their large, powerful shoulders.

Aurochs' horns were prized drinking vessels. Divine women offering heroes and gods drinking horns of mead were commonly depicted on Old Norse artifacts. In the myths, the drink offered from these horns is called the Mead of Poetry, or Memory. This magical mead contained restorative properties and bestowed wisdom, and the drinking horn is the structure that enabled this divine wisdom to flow.

The strength of Uruz With Fehu (pages 26–27), we spoke of the primal cow Auðumbla, who licked the first god to life from a block of ice. With Uruz, we might consider the god who emerged from the ice, Buri. Just as the aurochs were the giant ancestors of modern cattle, so Buri was immense and beautiful and was a father-ancestor to the gods. In *Gylfaginning*, part of *Snorri's Edda*, the goddess Gefjun, meaning "she who gives," employed four giant oxen to carve out a huge piece of land and

28 MEETING THE RUNES

drag it out to sea, creating the island of Sjaelland. Gefjun's oxen display the formative power, strength, and endurance that define this rune.

Uruz in the rune poems The rune poems all share different aspects of Uruz. The Anglo-Saxon rune poem reveres the aurochs' fearless fierceness and their ability to roam across vast moorlands. In the Old Norse poem, aurochs are replaced by reindeer, which were also a source of abundance and could traverse long distances across treacherous landscapes. However, in Iceland, where there were neither native aurochs nor reindeer, the rune's meaning took on a different form.

The Icelandic poem speaks of "drizzle," which gives Uruz its watery connection. Water is an enduring and strong element, which, over time, has the power to shape all life. We are mostly made of water, and so our survival and vitality depend upon it. When deep emotions arise, water manifests as tears, which heal and soothe the soul.

Reversed rune The Uruz rune reversed could represent a well that holds life-giving waters. This brings us to the Norn, Urðr, who dwells by Urðarbrunnr, the well of fate, and is one of the most enduring and mysterious beings in Old Norse cosmology.

Although Uruz's associations may differ, they do have core aspects in common. They all represent enduring strength, fundamental power, and the ability to form and shape the land.

Aurochs' horns would have been used for rituals, blessings, and group celebrations

URUZ IN PRACTICE

Although we are unable to witness a stampeding herd of aurochs, we can get a sense of their sacred wildness through bison or Highland cattle. Historically, hunting aurochs may have been a rite of passage and a test of skill. Today, our rites of passage could involve moving house, having interviews and meetings, starting a business, or doing anything that requires strength and confidence.

We can work with Uruz when we need to face challenges or opportunities head-on. Uruz is not necessarily the rune of quick fixes, but of having the power and stamina to stay the course. We feel Uruz in our bodies as grounding strength, power, and vitality surging through our veins.

As you chant Uruz, feel the energy of the earth and the hooves of hundreds of animals stampeding. Allow this rune to be a declaration of your primal power.

Divination meanings

- Uruz represents a time for strength, confidence, and endurance; to power up and face situations head-on.
- It reminds us to connect with the earth and feel the energy rise in our bodies.
- This rune brings healing and determination and encourages us to celebrate and "toast" ourselves and others.
- If we are feeling ill or unsure, Uruz gives us the courage to know that we have the strength to pull through.

By drumming, chanting, or stamping the floor, we can raise Uruz's power

30 MEETING THE RUNES

Bloodied by thorn runes
I sleep deep through the wounding
High on Hindarfjall

Thurisaz (thur-ree-sarz)

Thundering into the rune row with the power of Thor's hammer and a stampede of giants, Thurisaz holds the energy of a sharp rock jutting up from the quaking earth, a lightning strike, and a rockfall. It is a reminder of nature's ability to harm as well as heal.

Keywords: Giant, Thorn, Aggression, Boundaries, Protection, Power
Letter (Sound): Th
Deities: Giants, Thor, Loki
Elements: Fire, Water
Colors: Red, Black, Purple
Animals: Snake, Goat, Wolf
Trees & Plants: Rose, Thorn Tree, Bramble
Crystals & Minerals: Black Tourmaline, Sapphire, Lava Stone

Varied meanings Thurisaz means "giant" in the Old Norse rune poem and "thorn" in the Anglo-Saxon poem. The rune's shape is suggestive of Thor's hammer, Mjölnir, and of a sharp thorn, both of which have the power to defend and attack. Thurisaz is often viewed with caution as a rune of misfortune and aggression. Even though it does hold these meanings, it can also teach us rich and powerful lessons about primal wisdom, boundaries, and protection.

Thor's hammer, Mjölnir, was not only a weapon, but was also used in blessing rituals

THURISAZ 31

A rune of giants The giants, or *jötnar*, are integral to the Old Norse creation myths, and their complex and often antagonistic relationship with the gods is the basis of many mythological dramas and adventures. Contrary to popular belief, there is little mention in the texts of giants being necessarily large. They are, however, connected with primal and meteorological forces, wilderness, and chthonic wisdom. Although the male giants were usually described as unattractive and dangerous, the giantesses were often deemed beautiful, and they made desirous marriage matches for the gods.

According to the Eddas, the earth itself was created from the flesh of the first giant, Ymir, and the sky was made from his skull. Yes, that does mean that clouds were created from his brains! These tales imply that we are surrounded by the giants. They form the bones of the world, and their blood is the turbulent depths of the oceans. Thurisaz holds these volatile and primordial elements in its core.

Hammer and thorn Thurisaz is also connected with the giant-killing god, Thor, who is the strongest of all the gods and keeps the giants out of Asgard using his hammer, Mjölnir. When Thor throws the hammer, as well as cracking open the skulls of his enemies, it generates thunder and lightning and always returns to him like a booming boomerang. Mjölnir was also able to bestow divine blessings. In the poem *Þrymskviða*, from the *Poetic Edda*, the hammer was placed in the bride's lap to consecrate a marriage, and in *Snorri's Edda*, Thor was able to bring one of his goats back to life using Mjölnir's power.

As a rune of thorns, we see Thurisaz in the fairy tale of Sleeping Beauty. Not only did the princess prick her finger, sending her to sleep, but she was also surrounded by thornbushes, which shielded her from the outside world. An earlier sleep-thorn tale is told in the poem *Sigrdrífumál*, from the *Poetic Edda*, where the Valkyrie Sigrdrífa, trapped in the mountain Hindarfjall, was pricked by Odin's sleep-thorn for going against his wishes. She was not shielded by thorns but by a ring of fire.

The *jötnar* were typically enemies of the gods, though some acted as allies

THURISAZ IN PRACTICE

Thurisaz's association with thorns helps us to understand its power in our lives. Thorns protect the soft fruits that grow within the bushes, and thorn walls have long been used to create barriers between places. Conversely, the protection that thorns provide can also restrict growth and change, ensnaring those caught in the thorny grasp.

We feel Thurisaz in a rush of anger, in an impulsive desire to protect, and when we feel wounded and lash out. Thurisaz is a warning of outer and inner aggression, and often comes up when we hurt ourselves with our own thoughts and deeds. When required, it is effective at protection. However, just like Mjölnir returns to Thor, Thurisaz will return to you like a boomerang, so send it out only if you are prepared to catch its return. On a brighter note, Thurisaz can also represent crafts like metalwork and blacksmithing.

Chanting Thurisaz is raw and visceral and is best saved for moments of true need.

Divination meanings

- A warning that disruptive forces are at hand, Thurisaz is an emergency defense, highlighting the need to clear space and create solid boundaries.
- Thurisaz represents strong emotions that threaten to erupt at any moment.
- It embodies the challenge that makes us stronger, and the storm that clears the way for better things.
- This rune is a call to power and a warning against impulsive anger.
- It also reminds us that the thorn can turn inward when we harbor damaging thoughts about ourselves.

I am a whisper of streams as one-eyed screams
Ecstasy beyond death, a revelation in breath

Ansuz (arn-sooz)

The literal meaning of Ansuz is "god," and it is a rune of intellect, wisdom, and communication.

Keywords: Communication, Wisdom, Breath, Inspiration, Poetry, Divination
Letter: A
Deities: Odin, the Æsir
Elements: Air, Water
Colors: All Shades of Blue
Animals: Raven, Wolf, Eagle
Trees & Fungi: Ash, Fly Agaric
Crystals & Minerals: Lapis Lazuli, Sodalite

Odin's rune Although Ansuz is associated with all the Æsir gods, it is primarily Odin's rune. Ansuz connects with Odin's roles as a god of creation, wisdom, and ecstasy. It is a rune that opens the way for communion with deities and it is the first rune that expresses and explores divine mysteries. Odin's initiatory discovery of the runes is described in the poem *Hávamál*, from the *Poetic Edda*. After nine nights of self-sacrifice upon the windswept branches of Yggdrasil, Odin took up the runes, and as he did, he screamed. This scream feels like a defining moment, a piercing revelation into the night air, shifting reality. For Odin, this acquisition of numinous wisdom could only be expressed via the voice and he went on to share this wisdom with humanity.

Another meaning for Ansuz is "mouth," and at the heart of this rune are the powers of breath and sound. The first humans, Ask and Embla, were created out of driftwood by three wandering gods, Odin, Hœnir, and Lóðurr. It was Odin who gave them the gift of breath, and therefore life, by breathing into the wood.

Ansuz is the rune of leaders, and of poets, storytellers, singers, and seers. Poetry was so important to Odin that he went to great lengths to obtain the Mead of Poetry from the giant Suttungr, transforming himself into a snake, a man, and an eagle to accomplish his goal. The shape of Ansuz is suggestive of Odin's windswept cloak or perhaps of his hat tilted over his missing eye.

A gateway of wisdom In the Old Norse rune poem, Ansuz means "estuary." Estuaries are spaces where salt water flows into river mouths and fresh water flows out to the sea. The Vikings were well-acquainted with seafaring, and estuaries would have represented beginnings and endings of journeys. Estuaries are permeable gateways where we can gather wisdom and treasures from the ocean, and where our own stories become entwined with the vast tapestry of the seas.

ANSUZ IN PRACTICE

The simplest way of connecting with Ansuz is through the breath. By listening to the rhythmic flow of our breathing, we can calm the chatter of our minds and connect more deeply with our environment and with ourselves. Our breath enables us to transform air into life-giving energy, movement, and sound. Meditating on this can teach us a lot about the power of Odin's rune.

As a rune of communication, Ansuz helps us to express ourselves with clarity and conviction. Our voices have the power to change our reality, and in turn to make powerful changes in the world around us. It is also a reminder of the importance of listening and being open to learning new things. Odin's continual quest for knowledge is reflected in the Ansuz rune, which asks us to remain open to wisdom, vision, and wonder.

By creating an altar or a sacred space in our homes, we make space in our lives for communion with the gods. Creating an altar can be a joyful way of understanding our own relationship with the divine. As a rune of ecstatic experience, we can connect with Ansuz by shamanic drumming, dancing, breath work, or visiting places that inspire the soul.

Intoning Ansuz feels like a current of fresh air and flowing clear water. Chanting Ansuz clears the mind and brings calm clarity to deep matters.

Divination meanings

- Ansuz in a reading is an indication that important messages are coming through for you. Listen to your intuition and be open to signs and symbols in your daily life.
- This rune also signals a time of learning and opening your mind to new opportunities.
- When Ansuz appears, significant decisions could be at hand. Remember to align with your inner truth, and speak with integrity.
- Whether you are drawn to singing, writing, public speaking, or the path of the poet, Ansuz encourages you to focus on the magic and power of your voice.

I ride where hoofbeat unbinds heartbeat
And drumming opens the road
To a dreaming rhythm of stars

Raidho (ray-dough/ray-though)

As the rune of journeying, Raidho's literal meanings are "to ride," "riding," and "journey."

Keywords: Journey, Rhythm, Ride, Integration, Order, Harmony
Letter: R
Deities: Thor, Hermóðr, Odin
Elements: Air, Earth
Colors: Red, Blue
Animals: Horse, Goat
Trees & Plants: Oak, Mugwort
Crystals & Minerals: Selenite, Aventurine

The first half of this Ætt explored the forging of elemental powers, creation, and consciousness. Now we begin to integrate these energies and embark upon our own sacred adventures.

Raidho in the rune poems The Old Norse and Icelandic rune poems speak of a journey as the horse's hardship and the rider's happiness, whereas the Anglo-Saxon poem remarks upon the ease of discussing a journey while sat comfortably at home, as opposed to the challenges of riding long distances on horseback. Contemplating action is simple, but Raidho represents the courage to step out of the door and make it so.

Horses in Norse mythology Before motorized transport, horses were the only means of swift travel across long distances. Viking Age people were also well-known for traveling by boat, and a common kenning for ships were "horses" or "steeds of the sea." In the Old Norse creation myths, horses not only carried humans across the world, but guided celestial bodies and held the rhythms of the universe in place. Day (Dagr) and Night (Nótt) were pulled across the sky by the mythical horses Skinfaxi and Hrímfaxi, while the horses Árvakr and Alsviðr led the sun across the sky, their manes radiating sunlight, all while being chased by a huge, devouring wolf.

Odin and Sleipnir There are several mythic poems where horses were ridden into other worlds, often to Hel, the land of the dead. Odin's eight-legged steed Sleipnir was the preferred mount for such a treacherous ride. His eight legs not only made the journey swifter, but perhaps allowed for easier traveling between the worlds. *Baldrs draumar*, from the *Poetic Edda*, describes how Odin rides to Hel to uncover the meaning of his son Baldr's distressing nightmares. As he rides into Hel's misty realms, the poem mentions the resounding sound of Sleipnir's hooves.

The rhythmical beat of hooves could resemble the sound of a drum as shamanic drumming can create altered states of consciousness which facilitate journeys of the mind and soul. As the horse carries the body, repetitive drumbeats can carry the soul to other worlds. These shamanic journeys enable healing and provide opportunities to gain wisdom and understanding. Raidho has been found inscribed all over an Anglo-Saxon cremation urn, perhaps as a symbol of the deceased's journey to the afterlife.

Other deities connected with Raidho

This rune is also associated with Hermóðr and Thor. Hermóðr, who was the son of Odin and his wife Frigg, rode Sleipnir into Hel on Frigg's request; and Thor, the rambunctious god of thunder and agriculture, rode between the worlds on his chariot, pulled by two goats, Tanngrisnir and Tanngnjóstr.

Sleipnir played an intrinsic role in Odin's journeys between the worlds

RAIDHO IN PRACTICE

We have spoken of long journeys and vast cosmic themes, but our journey with Raidho begins right here, with the rhythm of our own beating hearts. This rune is the call to dance, to sing, and to find joy in life's journey. Remember to find space in your day for dance, for movement, and for song. Raidho is also about the small rituals that create powerful changes. One step at a time, it reminds us that it is our everyday actions that forge the rhythm of progress in our lives.

This rune is the excitement of planning a trip, and the road you travel along. It is the vehicle that carries you, and the adventures you have along the way. Inscribing Raidho upon your vehicle, tickets, suitcase, or passport is a blessing for safe travels and an ally for overcoming obstacles. We often rush from one place to another, but Raidho is an invitation to savor the journey itself.

Chanting Raidho is a resonance from our chest, out onto the road, reaching high mountains and deep rivers. It is a call to adventure, and a yearning for the quest to begin.

Divination meanings

- In a reading, Raidho indicates a time for travel, adventures, and an opportunity to expand horizons. Both physical and astral journeys are favored and bring a greater perspective.
- Raidho represents forward motion and highlights decisions about the path ahead. Tune in to your personal rhythms and move with the dance of life. Drumming, dancing, and song encourage visions and healings.
- If this rune comes up when questioning your spiritual path, it can signify that rituals and visionary journeys may be helpful in your connection with the divine.
- Raidho is a reminder to enjoy the ride!

I illuminate minds, extinguish the dark
I awaken desire, the forging of hearts
I leap from the pyre and pass on the spark

Kenaz (keh-naz)

As a rune of fire, Kenaz embodies the human expressions of the element. It also represents the channeling of raw, primal fire into a more controllable form, such as a torch, which is one of the rune's original meanings.

Keywords: Fire, Creativity, Knowledge, Wound, Illumination, Transformation
Letters: K, C
Deities: Freyja, Bragi, Wayland
Element: Fire
Colors: Orange, Red, Yellow, Blue, Black
Animals: Dragon, Phoenix, Firefly, Owl
Tree: Pine
Oils: Pine, Cinnamon, Frankincense, Ginger
Crystals & Minerals: Citrine, Carnelian, Bloodstone

The power of Kenaz The shape of Kenaz depicts fire coming from a torch, but it could also be viewed as the expansion or concentration of energy. Where Raidho (pages 36–38) brought rhythm, Kenaz bucks the trend by igniting something new. It is the artist's inspiration, the writer's spark, the adventurer's impulse to leap unknown into the dark. Kenaz is a multifaceted rune, stirring the creative juices, firing passions, cleansing, and illuminating, yet it also has the power to burn, destroy, and wound.

At its warm core, this rune speaks of creativity. Not only does Kenaz bring inspiration, but it also denotes the courage to create, and the dedication this is required to become adept at a craft. From a blacksmith to a wordsmith, the light and heat of Kenaz acts as a forge of transformation for all kinds of creative processes.

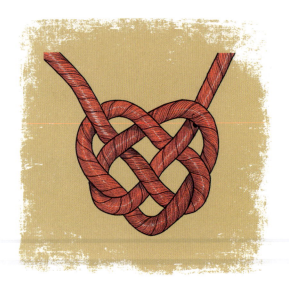

Kenaz in the rune poems In the Anglo-Saxon rune poem, Kenaz is a bright fire, whereas the Old Norse poem speaks of it meaning "ulcer," and of being a danger to children. The danger of fiery Kenaz is in swellings, infections, and fevers. However, fevers are the body's way of fighting infection, and swellings protect our bones from further injury, meaning Kenaz could be seen as both the illness and the cure.

The deities connected with Kenaz In the Old Norse mythologies, Kenaz is associated with the legendary creators, such as Wayland the Smith, who was married to a swan maiden and created the most beautiful jewels imaginable. Unfortunately, Wayland was captured and wounded by a cruel and greedy king, and he went on to exact a terrible revenge, killing the king's sons. With his incredible artisanry, Wayland then crafted mechanical wings and flew away from his captors. In England, there are several places named after Wayland, including Wayland's Smithy, a Neolithic long barrow in Oxfordshire.

Of the Æsir gods, it is Bragi who is named the god of poetry. He is a wise, eloquent, harp-playing god, married to the goddess Iðunn, who is exceptionally important to all the gods, because she owns the apples of immortality. From this marriage, poetry is intertwined with immortality and holds the keys to eternal youth. In the poem *Sigrdrífumál*, from the *Poetic Edda*, the Valkyrie Sigrdrífa speaks of rune spells being carved on to gods, animals, and objects. She mentions that runes were carved upon Bragi's tongue, which creates an interesting vision of the runes activating Bragi's magical words.

Freyja's magic is woven throughout the first Ætt, and within Kenaz's fire she is a creatrix of magic and a goddess of passion. In *Gylfaginning*, part of *Snorri's Edda*, Snorri expresses that Freyja is fond of love poetry.

40 MEETING THE RUNES

KENAZ IN PRACTICE

Whenever a sense of adventure excites you, Kenaz is calling. When the desire to create stirs within, Kenaz is igniting. When mixing colors on a palette, Kenaz is warming. When studies illuminate your mind, Kenaz is shining; and when a fever fills your body, Kenaz is cleansing.

This rune is present wherever there is creativity, enlightenment, and transformation. You can connect with Kenaz while studying, cooking, learning a new craft, or when you need the fire and focus to persist with a project. If you are feeling stuck in life, Kenaz reignites the fire of inspiration and sheds new light on your path. Kenaz is in the book that changed your life and in the brushstrokes of a painting that began to heal your wounded heart.

Chanting Kenaz feels like a bright, cleansing, and invigorating light.

Divination meanings

- Kenaz signifies a time of creativity, illumination, and study, and encourages us to follow our inspiration or learn something new.
- In a reading, Kenaz can mean healing, cleansing, and transformation. Although transformation ultimately leads to enlightenment, it can often be a challenging path.
- This rune can sometimes be a sign of an illness or wounding.

I will meet you here, rooted to earth
Open to heaven, a kiss between the worlds

Gebo (geh-bo)

The meaning of Gebo is "gift," and it is a rune of giving and exchange.

Keywords: Giving, Gift, Friendship, Reciprocity, Promise, Sacrifice
Letter: G
Deities: Odin, Gefjun, Freyja
Elements: Air, Earth
Colors: Blue, Gold
Animals: Ox, Raven, Wolf
Trees: Ash, Elm
Oil: Patchouli
Crystals & Minerals: Citrine, Gold, Lapis Lazuli, Rose Quartz

Gifts and sacrifices Gift-giving was a fundamental aspect of Old Norse culture, and it encompassed more than the simple exchange of physical gifts. Reciprocity was part of the strict honor codes that governed Viking Age society, signifying alliances and solidifying communities. In the poem *Hávamál*, from the *Poetic Edda*, Odin states the importance of gift-giving among friends, however Gebo also signifies divine exchanges between humans and the gods.

For millennia, people have visited temples and ritual sites to commune with the gods, making offerings and sacrifices in hope of winning favor, blessings, and protection. These sacrifices have included food and drink, jewelry, weapons, and pottery, as well as animal, and sometimes human, sacrifice. A sacrifice is given in the hope that a prayer will be answered, and in these moments, we open up to commune with the divine. Gebo represents this magical meeting point, and speaks of a balanced connection between two energies, with both sides giving and receiving in equal measure. Gebo is shaped like the crossing of two roof beams, offering shelter and support from the elements. The exchange of Gebo is also connected with the promise of marriage, making it a rune of serious romantic connections and betrothals.

Gebo in the source texts Of the three rune poems, Gebo only appears in the Anglo-Saxon rune poem, which praises generosity as an honorable trait that should be extended to all.

In *Gylfaginning*, part of *Snorri's Edda*, King Gylfi offered the goddess Gefjun as much land as she could plow in exchange for the pleasure of her company. We read in Uruz (pages 28–30) what a misjudgment Gylfi made. Gefjun's oxen plowed so hard that the land broke away, forming an island, which she took with her.

Perhaps this story is a lesson in the benefits of knowing the full terms and conditions before promising an exchange! Gefn, "giver," is also a title for Freyja in her role as goddess of abundance.

Odin is known to give gifts, and rewards those who die in battle with a place in his realm, Valhalla. In the *Saga of the Volsungs*, Odin appeared one night at the king's hall and thrusted a magnificent sword into a tree, saying that whoever could pull the sword out could keep it. Like the story of the sword in the stone, only the worthy hero Sigmund was able to retrieve it.

GEBO IN PRACTICE

Gebo is a very relevant rune for our modern lives, which we probably use every day without realizing! As a gift of affection, we sign off communications to our loved ones with at least one "X." When agreeing to a contract, we sign by the "X," and when locating something of importance we use the phrase "X marks the spot."

Some of us find it easy to give, but harder to receive, and Gebo invites us to address this imbalance. Paying attention to our breathing can help us with this. If we exhale without allowing an inhale, we soon get into trouble.

Gebo is the reminder of the promise we did not fulfill, and the desire to give back to those who have shown us generosity. In our spiritual lives, Gebo represents our desire to reach out to the divine, to give gratitude, and honor the presence of wonder in our lives. It is an offering at the altar, and a reminder that the most precious gift we can give to someone is time and presence.

Chanting Gebo is expansive, opening us up to the mystery of life. It feels like the balance of giving and of surrender.

Divination meanings

- Gebo represents a time of giving and receiving, and of offering up your own gifts to the world.
- It could be a sign to connect with a lover, or a suggestion of engagements and marriage.
- This rune also indicates the signing of contracts for work or for a new home and encourages us to be true to our word.
- Gebo loves random acts of kindness and generosity, and is a rune that represents our own relationship with the divine.

Your arms cast amber light around me
Resting upon a mountain edge of charm
I open my wings to the dissolving sun

Wunjo (woon-yoh)

As we reach the final joyful rune of the first Ætt, Wunjo represents harmonious union with our family, friends, communities, and lovers.

Keywords: Joy, Celebration, Prosperity, Pleasure, Fulfillment, Victory
Letter: W
Deities: Odin, Frigg, Freyja, Freyr
Elements: Earth, Air
Colors: White, Yellow, Amber, Gold, Purple
Animals: Dragonfly, Butterfly, Wolf, Stag, Boar
Trees: Ash, Chestnut
Oils: Neroli, Orange
Crystals & Minerals: Aventurine, Citrine, Diamond

A blissful rune Wunjo completes the creative and elemental energies of Freyja and Freyr's Ætt. This rune looks like a flag, a weather vane, and a compass point. As a flag, it is the joy of our clan and the pride of who we are. As a weather vane, it is the wind in our sails gliding us quickly across smooth waters, or the exhilaration of surfing a wave. As a compass point, it is the feeling of being directed on your soul's path and is perhaps the original seed of the saying, "follow your bliss."

Wunjo is a rune of belonging and harmony. It is the binding force that holds tribes, families, and friends together. For our ancestors, being part of a tribe or clan meant safety and health. Today, it is still important for us to remember that we are not islands and that the glue of community can bring us unexpected joys and support.

Joy and sorrow Of the three rune poems, it is only the Anglo-Saxon rune poem that mentions Wunjo, and speaks of joy and the absence of sorrows. This absence of sorrow is apt for this point in the Ætt, because we are about to embark upon an Ætt of challenges and growth.

Joy and sorrow are two sides of the same coin; if we knew only joy, it would lose its meaning, and too much sorrow dulls the heart to knowing bliss. Herein lies the ache of Wunjo. It is daring to love, whether requited or not; it is loving so deeply, even though one day you know you will lose it; it is the climax and vulnerability of sex; it is the peak of the mountain without knowing what is on the other side. It is the courage to follow your soul's compass even though it means leaving behind that which you once called home.

Reputation in the Viking Age Home and reputation are also things that the Anglo-Saxon rune poem mentions as bringing happiness and security. In the Viking Age, a good reputation was one of the most valuable qualities to possess and maintain. The state of your reputation would affect your social and economic status, as well as your relationships and legal standing. In the poem *Hávamál*, from the *Poetic Edda*, Odin affirms the importance of a good reputation because it never dies. He later speaks of a rune that attracts the object of his desire to him. This could indeed be referring to the power of Wunjo as a rune of attraction and sexuality. Wunjo embodies genuine mutual attraction and is not aligned with harmful and deceptive love magic.

WUNJO IN PRACTICE

We experience Wunjo within joyful community; friends who feel like family, and families that bring support and comradery. This rune is a blessing and a celebration. It is remembering and honoring all that we are grateful for and proud of. It is the celebration of our achievements: the graduation, initiation, and promotion. It is the warmth, relief, and comfort of a home.

We feel Wunjo in the excitement of attraction and within sensual pleasure. This rune is the hopeful feeling of everything going our way, and the potential of what success could bring. It is the blessing of groups working harmoniously together, and we also find Wunjo in the golden light of the setting sun, which fills our hearts with joy. The transience of Wunjo makes the joy even more potent. It is a rune that binds things and people together, making it a wonderful rune to work in to bind runes (two or more runes combined into a single symbol) and spellcraft.

Intoning Wunjo feels like warmth, celebration, attainment, and laughter.

Divination meanings

- In a reading, Wunjo can mean a celebration, a success, and a sense of achievement.
- It suggests a relationship could be blossoming, or that longing will be fulfilled.
- Wunjo is a sign that all kinds of love and companionship surround the querent.
- This rune brings hope and relief and indicates that everything will work out well.

THE SECOND ÆTT

Heimdall's Ætt

The second Ætt embodies the challenges and changes that can facilitate deep transformation. Wild natural forces surge through this Ætt, shaking our sense of equilibrium and revealing the strength and depth of our essential, shining nature.

This Ætt is commonly known as Heimdall's Ætt, but it is also called Hel's or Hagall's Ætt and I believe the row relates to all three titles.

Heimdall is the trusted watchman of the gods and the guardian of Bifröst, the rainbow bridge that joins Midgard and Asgard. He has golden teeth, shining armor, and possesses extraordinarily acute senses. He can hear grass growing in the fields and see far into the distance, even at night. At the first signs of Ragnarök, Heimdall blew his mighty Gjallarhorn, alerting the gods to the impending battle. Because Heimdall guards the bridge between the worlds, this Ætt could be seen as a bridge between the first and third Ætt.

Queen Hel is the daughter of the god Loki and the *jötunn* Angrboða. She presides over the realm of the dead, which is also called Hel, or Helheim. The word "Hel" means "hidden" or "covered" and is thought to be a place where those who died of natural causes dwell. Unlike the latter Christian hell, it was not a place of punishment, but more of a continuation of life after death. Queen Hel is usually portrayed with a face that is half beautiful and half blue, the color of the dead. Like the duality of her appearance, she can be both fierce and tender. Odin, fearing the children of Loki, threw her into Niflheim, which she took over and became Queen. As a goddess of facing shadows and overcoming hardships, her influence over this Ætt is hard to deny.

The title Hagall's Ætt is self-explanatory, because the row begins with the Hagalaz rune (pages 48–50), and these two names are interchangeable. You do not have to connect with a deity to work with the runes and, as you will discover, Hagalaz holds the seed of ancient magic.

This row may contain some challenging runes, but as you get to know them, I hope you will discover their rich, healing power. Each rune contains multifaceted meanings and, alongside destruction, this rune row brings divine protection, and guardianship, guiding us on the path of empowerment and initiation.

A sharp torrent breaks the sky gray
Mother Storm washes away
A roaring seed, surrendered within

Hagalaz (har-gahl-arz)

We begin the second Ætt with the shrill call of inescapable change. Hagalaz arrives with the shock of a sudden hailstorm, and it may depart just as quickly, leaving our world utterly transformed.

Keywords: Hail, Disruption, Seed, Winter, Bridge, Sudden Change
Letter: H
Deities: Hel/Hella, Holda/Holle, Urðr, Heimdall, Ymir, Móðguðr
Element: Water
Colors: Gray, Blue, White
Trees: Ash, Yew
Crystals & Minerals: Clear Quartz, Ice Crystals

A rune of destruction and chaos At face value, Hagalaz represents destructive and chaotic powers that can bring delays, disruptions, and adversity. Another name for this rune is Hagall, meaning "hail." Just as a hailstorm can decimate a field of crops, so Hagalaz can throw our lives into unexpected chaos. Hagalaz is not an easy rune, but it is a necessary one that clears the way for better times to come. At the sparkling heart of this icy rune is a powerful seed of deep transformation and the hope of something new.

The deities associated with Hagalaz
Hagalaz is associated with some formidable, divine women: Hel, Holda, and Urðr. Hel rules the realm of the dead and she is a multifaceted goddess who commands respect. Depending on how we approach her, Hel can appear cold and fearful, or tender and loving. Her face demonstrates this duality, with one side appearing dead, and the other vibrant and beautiful. Hagalaz shares this complexity, bringing both fear and healing, disruption and transformation.

Holda, also known as Frau Holle, is a goddess connected with winter and the underworld. She was thought to bring the first snowflakes of the year, and heralds the icy transformation of winter. Holda lovingly guides the souls of deceased infants to the afterlife via her sacred well. As one of the leaders of the Wild Hunt, she rides across the winter skies, leading a wild horde of mythological beings. Holda weaves both life and death, and represents the necessary and headling aspects of this rune.

Urðr is one of the Norns who we will meet several times on our runic journey. She is an ancient being who holds all past knowledge and tends Yggdrasil with the healing waters from the well of fate. From this flowing water, all things become green and fertile, which is reminiscent of the effects of meltwater after a storm.

Both being guardians of bridges between the worlds, Móðguðr and Heimdall are also associated with this rune, because the shape of Hagalaz can be seen as a bridge.

Hagalaz in the rune poems The rune poems equate Hagalaz to hail, a destructive, cold, white grain. The Old Icelandic poem speaks of the sickness that hail and sleet can cause, whereas the Old Norse poem has an odd-sounding line about Christ shaping the heavens. This is likely to be a later Christian modification, with Christ replacing an older deity. However, it does speak of the rune's ability to create as well as to destroy. The Anglo-Saxon poem mentions hail melting into water, reminding us that even though hail brings destruction, it also contains the water that nourishes the land.

Hel is the goddess primarily associated with Hagalaz

HAGALAZ IN PRACTICE

We can experience the physical shock of Hagalaz when we are caught out in a hailstorm, and when safely ensconced in our homes, we can hear the hail sharply hitting the windows. While writing the text for this section of the book, there have been hailstorms every few hours, and I observed the changeability of the tumultuous skies. One minute, the world is dark and brooding; the next, a clear blue sky opens up to hope.

Hagalaz is a rune of winter's beginnings, and although this implies some inherent discomfort or danger, it also allows space for stillness, reflection, and deep inner work. We can experience this rune while observing nature in a wintry landscape, when the empty bones of trees point to the heavens and the land is frozen beneath our feet.

We feel Hagalaz when we are shocked, and when we are hit by sudden, undesirable changes. Although it often relates to adverse external forces, this rune can also be indicative of the painful chaos within our own minds.

Chanting this rune feels like hail beating down on a window. As Thurisaz (pages 31–33) was raw and visceral, so Hagalaz has a guttural sound of gravel and ice. This rune can be used for protection in dire straits, or as a form of attack.

Divination meanings

- This rune signals necessary disruption and change; shocks that lead to transformation. Even if life feels chaotic, there is a seed of hope within the storm.
- Hagalaz can represent a time of solitude and reflection.
- It marks a period of upheaval leading to healing and new understanding.

I see you now, fall to the ground
Whisper my name, into the land

Nauthiz (north-eez)

This rune follows on from Hagalaz like hunger follows a bad harvest, and represents the absolute bare bones of necessity.

Keywords: Need, Hunger, Necessity, Desire, Resistance
Letter: N
Deity: Skuld
Element: Fire
Colors: Black, Red
Trees: Beech, Rowan
Crystals & Minerals: Clear Quartz, Pyrite, Fire Agate, Lava

Need and necessity The literal meanings of Nauthiz are "need" and "necessity," and although it is a challenging rune, it is not a passive one. Nauthiz is the kindled "need-fire" of survival, which illuminates the gaping void between where we are in life and where we need to be. It is also the fire that drives us forward, toward who we will become. We can hear Nauthiz in the old saying, "necessity is the mother of invention" and see it in the movie *Gone with the Wind* when Scarlett O'Hara shakes her fist at the sky, claiming she will "never be hungry again!"

Threads of fate The first three runes of this Ætt are deeply entwined with the Norns and therefore connect with inescapable aspects of fate. Skuld, the Norn who cuts the threads and speaks of what shall be, is associated with Nauthiz. Some threads in life's tapestry are absolute and cannot be changed, whereas some can be reimagined and rewoven. The shape of Nauthiz is evocative of a thread being rewoven or cut. Skuld is also mentioned in several poems to be a Valkyrie, collecting slain warriors from the battlefield. She is the only Norn actively moving around in the world, exemplifying the determined movement that Nauthiz requires.

Hardship and desire The hardships of winter and poverty are mentioned in the Old Norse rune poem, whereas the Icelandic poem speaks of another type of Viking Age hardship, which was the terrible and all-too-common case of being a bondwoman (enslaved woman). The Anglo-Saxon poem offers a little more hope because it focuses on opportunities to receive help and to improve our situation.

The purpose of Nauthiz isn't to point out the obvious or to rub salt in the wound, but to encourage action that will prevent toxic issues from repeating. Nauthiz is not only the pang of hunger, but also the ache of desire. This rune can represent those times when pleasure and pain cross over, and when the need-fire burns for someone you long for.

NAUTHIZ IN PRACTICE

In a world of ever-increasing distractions, Nauthiz cuts away the unnecessary noise to reveal our true needs and desires. Its appearance is a sign to slow down and reconsider our thoughts and actions. Do we need to cut ties with a certain person or situation? Would a journey or venture benefit from greater planning? Is our behavior helping or hindering our progress?

This rune doesn't sugarcoat the truth, nor does it allow us to bypass the moments that hurt. Nauthiz does, however, offer aid to those who need it and forcefully creates space for us to reassess what is of true value in our lives. Nauthiz appears when we are out of sync with our integrity, and we experience this rune in the dark night of the soul and in the phoenix-like transformation it brings. Although Nauthiz is often viewed in a negative light, it is also a protector and makes a powerful ally on our path.

When I chant Nauthiz, the beginning part of the rune feels like a hollowing of the chest, whereas the "iz," or "eez," feels like a kindled fire or the arrival of needed support.

Divination meanings

- In a reading, Nauthiz can represent our immediate needs and the challenges we face in obtaining them.
- It indicates a time of lack or reflection that pushes us to reassess our direction in life.
- Nauthiz is the need to ask for help and support, and to cut away the distractions to focus on your goals.
- It kindles the fire of resilience that helps us to turn the tide on misfortune.
- This rune highlights the need to be aware of what we truly desire.

An invocation of frost
Wakes the spirits
Resting upon a frosted knife
A crystalline kingdom of ice

Isa (ee-sah)

As the last of the three winter runes that open this Ætt, Isa is a kinder rune than Hagalaz or Nauthiz and represents the stasis of winter.

Keywords: Ice, Stillness, Beauty, Patience, Introspection, Stasis
Letter: I
Deities: Verðandi, Skaði
Element: Water (Ice)
Colors: White, Blue
Animals: Reindeer, Arctic Fox, Bat, Serpent
Tree: Alder
Oil: Lavender
Crystals & Minerals: Clear Quartz, Selenite, Lace Agate, Blue Barite

A rune of ice Isa is a shining frost, the silence of a snow-covered landscape, and the intricate beauty of ice crystals. Ice slows everything down; water freezes, swellings reduce, and the activity of bacteria is paused. Ice is treacherous underfoot, and so we, too, must slow down and move carefully. Life rests beneath winter's ice, and Isa encourages us to do the same. Isa is the letter "I," a straight line that relates to a sense of self. It is a rune that helps us to build confidence and personal stability. If we stand as an Isa rune, we stand tall and proud. As a rune of quiet healing, Isa indicates a time to go within, to focus, and to reflect, but it can also represent emotional distance and coldness.

The glittering glamour of ice may be enchanting, but it will ultimately leave you cold. This cruelty is exemplified in the fairy tale *The Snow Queen*, where shards of an icy magical mirror become lodged in a young boy's heart and eyes, making him angry and cruel. He finds no joy in life apart from studying snowflakes with a magnifying glass. He is eventually healed only by the warm and loving tears of his friend who sobs over his heart.

Isa in the rune poems The Old Norse rune poem speaks of how ice creates a broad bridge. In the North, where winters are severe, frozen waters transform landscapes, and rivers become bridges. Although this can cause hardship, it has historically been a time of festivities such as frost fairs. The first recorded frost fair on the River Thames in London, UK, occurred in the Anglo-Saxon era, where stalls were set up on the ice and people ice-skated for work and play. Isa invites us to change our perspective and represents the blocks that may turn out to be blessings. The Old Norse poem mentions the need to care for the elderly and those in need, reminding us that winter requires community support for survival.

The Anglo-Saxon poem, which was composed in slightly gentler climes, speaks of the gem-like beauty of Isa; whereas the Old Icelandic poem highlights Isa's danger, saying that it is the downfall of doomed men. The idea that someone's doom is predetermined connects Isa to concepts of fate and to the Norn, Verðandi.

The deities associated with Isa Verðandi is the omnipresent weaving of time. Her name translates as "becoming" or "present." Of all the Norns, she is the most inscrutable, for when we try to grasp the moment it will always slip through our fingers. Practicing mindfulness and stillness are great ways to connect with Verðandi, Isa, and ourselves.

Another goddess connected with Isa is the *jötunn* goddess of skiing and hunting named Skaði. Her name means "harm," and she is associated with ice, snow, and wolves. The "harm" of Skaði is the danger of winter, but she is also a patron of skiers, and those who are drawn to icy, mountainous regions.

Verðandi, the Norn of the present, represents a time of pause and introspection

54 MEETING THE RUNES

ISA IN PRACTICE

We feel Isa when we pause and take time for ourselves. It is a rune of physical and spiritual stillness. Like the "in-between" days at the end of the year, Isa speaks of a "time out of time," and indicates creating space for retreat and integration. Isa offers more stability than the previous two runes; however, it is a dangerous space to remain for too long. Isa is a rune of the ego and is a positive rune for developing a stronger sense of self. This rune also warns against becoming stuck in our ways.

We experience Isa while in the majesty of a winter landscape and in the quiet of falling snow. Ice-skating or sledging are activities we can undertake to connect us with the playful and sometimes painful aspects of ice!

Isa is a high and soft note to chant, which feels like sunlight dancing on ice. The sound links to our higher self and creates a gentle sense of clarity.

Divination meanings

- In a reading, Isa indicates physical and spiritual stillness and stasis.
- It is a rune of the self and is helpful in defining who we are and what we value in life.
- Isa reminds us to enjoy the beauty of winter but to not lose ourselves to the slippery cold.
- This rune represents delays, blockages, or the need to take time out.
- Within relationships, it can be a difficult rune because it represents that someone is unable or unwilling to move forward.

Around the fire
We watch the ashes burn
As the old year turns

Jera (yeh-rah)

The wheel of the year turns and ice melts, heralding the return of spring. Jera is a sign of change and better times to come.

Keywords: Year, Harvest, Fruitfulness, Earth, Transformation, Time
Letter: J
Deities: Freyja, Freyr, Fródhi, Nerthus, Sif, Sumarr, Vetr, Sól, Máni
Element: Earth
Colors: Light Blue, Green, Brown, Gold
Animal: Eagle
Trees & Plants: Oak, Rosemary
Oil: Rosemary
Crystals & Minerals: Moss Agate, Citrine, Carnelian

Change and abundance Jera means "year" and encompasses all the seasons. It is the only rune with separate parts and marks the halfway point of the Elder Futhark. Its symbol is two Kenaz runes (pages 39–41), moving around a central axis. As a rune of agriculture, harvest, and the rewards of hard work, Jera marks a time of celebrating good fortune and the abundance of the earth. It represents the ripening corn and the sweetest fruit, and the accomplishments that bring us peace. Its duality reminds us that even if this year's crop is abundant, next year's harvest is never guaranteed.

The two sides of Jera represent the opposing forces of Sumarr and Vetr who are the Old Norse personifications of summer and winter. The seed of winter

56 MEETING THE RUNES

Jera reminds us to slow down and celebrate the fruitfulness of the earth

is stored within summer's bright heart, as the days begin to wane after the summer solstice. Likewise, the seed of summer is ignited on the darkest night of the winter solstice.

Jera is a rune of long-term planning. It is the deep magic of planting a seed in the dark earth and receiving sustenance in return. Just as nature can't be rushed, we must take our time with Jera.

Jera in the rune poems The Old Norse rune poem speaks of Fródhi's generosity. Fródhi was a legendary Danish king whose reign was a time of unprecedented peace. He is often considered to be a guise of the Vanir fertility god, Freyr. The peace of Fródhi was ensured by a magical mill named Grotti. This mill would churn out anything the miller commanded, and it was worked by two enslaved giantesses named Fenja and Menja. The king asked for gold, peace, and prosperity to be ground out, but he refused to give the women adequate rest. Growing tired of the abuse, the giantesses secretly ground out an army to oppose Fródhi, and thus he was killed and his time of peace ended.

This poem speaks of the blessings of peace and abundance, but it also provides a stark warning against greed and exploitation. The duality of Jera can be related to cause and effect, and the need to act in a balanced and harmonious way.

Both the Icelandic and Anglo-Saxon poems speak of the joys of an abundant harvest and the pleasure of plenty.

JERA IN PRACTICE

Nowadays, we can eat all kinds of foods regardless of the season and we usually have little to do with the tending or harvesting of our produce. This was not the case for people of the Viking Age, who often contended with harsh environmental conditions to carve out a living. Most of the Scandinavians who went out on Viking raids returned to farming after the raids were over. In our modern lives, Jera can help us live in greater harmony with the seasons and understand the cycles of our own lives. Using the story of Fródhi as a warning, the two balanced parts of Kenaz remind us of the importance of giving back to Mother Earth and the dangers of exploiting her.

Jera is writing down a dream and finding a way to achieve it. It is the sweet spot between hoping for the future and learning from the past. It's the work you put in and the payoff you receive. Jera is also a rune of gratitude and celebration, so remember to count your blessings and celebrate all your successes.

Chanting Jera is a joyful sound. It is a warm and high tone of success and the light of hope for what is to come.

Divination meanings

- This rune represents plans successfully being brought to fruition, and rewards for hard work. It is a sign you are on the right track to achieve your goals.
- Jera is a mark of natural change and the passage of time, and also signifies the magic of the seasons.
- It signals a time of abundance, harmony, and gentle healing.
- Jera highlights the need to keep life in balance and to consider the bigger picture. It denotes cause and effect, and completion.

My secrets are not for the light
I remain a keeper of night
I stand sentinel in between
I am wisdom evergreen

Eihwaz (aye-warz)

As the rune of the yew tree, Eihwaz symbolizes all its manifold mysteries.

Keywords: Renewal, Strength, Divination, Mysteries, Endurance, Protection
Letters: EI, AE, Y
Deities: Ullr, Skaði, Odin
Elements: Fire, Earth
Colors: Black, Brown, Dark Green, Red
Animals: Serpent, Eagle
Tree: Yew
Crystals & Minerals: Smoky Quartz, Ruby, Topaz

A rune of renewal Eihwaz is associated with the yew tree and reflects its qualities of renewal, strength, and resilience. Yew trees are renowned for their exceptional longevity and are able to live for thousands of years. Yew is an evergreen tree with wood that is hard, easy to flake, and slow to burn. These aspects are mentioned in the Anglo-Saxon and Old Norse rune poems. The Anglo-Saxon poem also speaks of the tree's twining roots, which are the keys to the yew's self-renewal. New shoots and branches can grow into the earth and form roots, which then become part of the main trunk.

Death and protection Yews are trees of death and represent the mysteries of the afterlife. Before we can renew, we must allow the old dead wood of our lives to fall away. Their presence in graveyards predates the churches built around them, as the early churches took over established places of worship. The yew's connection with death and protection is also evident in its prolific use in making ancient weapons, with the oldest longbow ever discovered being made from yew wood.

Although we usually think of Yggdrasil as an ash tree, it is also considered to be a yew. The yew's powerful connections to life, death, and rebirth make it a likely candidate as the evergreen world tree of Norse mythology.

Yew is exceptionally poisonous and must never be ingested. Despite its deadly nature, it also has healing properties and it is a wise teacher and guardian. Such is the power of yew that even resting under its bowers can cause trance-like experiences. The yew's ability to induce trance states connects Eihwaz with meditation and spiritual journeying.

The elongated and elegant shape of Eihwaz resembles a central column connecting the worlds, simultaneously reaching up to the heavens and anchoring down into the earth.

The deities associated with Eihwaz Ullr, the Old Norse god of winter, made his home in a place called Ýdalir, meaning Yewsdale. Ullr is associated with skiing and hunting and is usually depicted with a yew-wood bow and a quiver of arrows. Although there is little written about him in the texts, he was widely revered across Scandinavia because there are numerous places named after him, including Ullensaker in Norway. Some say that the winter huntress Skaði was originally Ullr's partner, and she also favored a yew-wood bow.

EIHWAZ IN PRACTICE

Eihwaz is the presence of death and rebirth in our lives. As yew endures by allowing the dead wood to fall, so Eihwaz teaches us to release all that no longer serves us and to trust the roots that nourish us.

It is a rune of the courage required to stand up for ourselves and to walk our own sacred path. Eihwaz is an invitation to face our fears and journey between the worlds. Its wisdom is as rich and deep as an ancient yew, and as quick as a hunter's arrow across the snow. Eihwaz comes to us when we are ready to be challenged and to be changed, but it also offers protection and the knowledge that we are not alone.

Eihwaz is a long call that feels like a gateway between the worlds. As I chant it, I feel it moving up and down my spine. It is a call of connection and a statement of being present here and now.

Divination meanings

- Eihwaz denotes a powerful time of transition and renewal. Courage and resilience are required but the rewards will be worth it.
- This rune indicates spiritual journeying, connecting with the divine and seeking wisdom.
- As a rune of protection, it is a sign that if you ask for help, you will be supported.
- Eihwaz is a guardian between the worlds, and in a reading, it can signify a willingness to understand life's greater mysteries.

All that shall be, trembles in memory
Precious threads, they weave and mend in me

Perthro (pur-throh)

The meaning of the word "Perthro" is unknown, although different ideas have been suggested, such as gaming pieces, cup, grave mound, fruit tree, and vagina, giving us powerful concepts to explore.

In Viking and Anglo-Saxon burials, men were often buried with cups, dice, and board games

Keywords: Destiny, Birth, Wyrd, Mystery, Chance, Cup
Letter: P
Deities: The Norns, Frigg, Iðunn
Element: Water
Colors: Silver, Black
Animal: Spider
Trees: Fruit Trees
Crystals & Minerals: Aquamarine, Hematite, Meteorite Stone

Gaming and fate Perthro is attested only in the Anglo-Saxon rune poem, which speaks of warriors playing and laughing in the beer hall. This has led many people to associate Perthro with gaming and fate. For the warriors in the beer hall, gaming was not just a fun pastime but a way of testing or demonstrating one's luck. The phrase "someone's luck has run out on them," refers to a Viking Age belief in luck spirits called *hamingjur*.

A person's *hamingja* is a female guardian spirit who has their own inherent agency, leaving or returning to a person at will. If a warrior repeatedly lost their games of dice or chess, it would be seen that their *hamingja* had deserted them and you would perhaps think twice about following them into battle.

Other associations Some rune scholars believe that Perthro relates to birthing more than gaming, and it could be envisioned that while the men were in the mead hall, some women would be tending to childbirth in their quarters. Childbirth in the Viking Age held huge risks for both mother and baby, linking Perthro once more to elements of fate and "luck." Perthro is not only the luck of an outcome, but the mysteries of creation and the magic of the process.

While Eihwaz (pages 59–60) relates to the yew, Perthro can be associated with fruit trees, particularly the magical apple tree belonging to the goddess Iðunn. The apples, which Iðunn keeps in a casket, rejuvenate the gods and maintain their youthfulness.

As a rune of fate and mystery, Perthro connects deeply with the Norns and their sacred well, Urðarbrunnr. I imagine it is only the Norns who fully comprehend the mysteries of Perthro.

The mystery of Perthro For me, Perthro represents that which cannot be expressed in words; the experiences so profound that words are brittle in comparison. I am not a mother, but I imagine that the experiences of childbirth and meeting the known unknown of your child transcend all description. Likewise, there are no words, in the English language at least, that describe those moments where you feel a rapture of the spirit, a glimpse between the veils, and a deepening connection with the divine. They simply just *feel* a certain way to us. For me, Perthro feels like a dark night illuminated by stars. It feels like the space between the roots of Yggdrasil. It feels like a deep silver pool, the ripples of which create patterns that flow into the tapestries of our lives, forever changing.

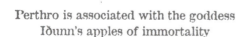

Perthro is associated with the goddess Iðunn's apples of immortality

PERTHRO IN PRACTICE

Although Perthro is connected with pregnancy and childbirth, it is a rune that encompasses everyone, no matter if we are parents or not. Perthro represents life's essential mysteries; it is a cauldron of memory, and the well of fate. We meet this rune when important decisions are to be made, or when we are seeking to reweave the threads of our lives. Although life's journey is filled with uncertainty, the presence of Perthro encourages us to dare to roll the dice and weave the dream.

Perthro represents the mysteries of creativity more than the things we create. It is the muse from the deep that brings a song to our lips, or the experience we try to encapsulate in a poem. Because it is shaped like a sideways container, Perthro can symbolize a circle of support.

Chanting Perthro is a low sound that opens us up to possibilities. Chanted gently, it can feel like entering a healing pool; chanted more powerfully, it could encourage a woman in labor.

Divination meanings

- The presence of Perthro in a reading can suggest something hidden being brought to light and secrets being revealed.
- It indicates an initiation of some kind, and a gateway into a new phase of life.
- This is a rune of the flow of *wyrd* (fate), cause, and effect, and it is an invitation to be comfortable with uncertainty and to be open to the great mysteries.

> White feathers around my neck
> White feathers surround me
> Swathed in light, dressed in night

Algiz (al-geez)

Also called Elhaz, Algiz is the ultimate rune of divine protection. Although it is attested in only one rune poem, it is one of the most complex runes of the second Ætt.

The shape of Algiz is reminiscent of a swan's foot

Keywords: Protection, Defense, Blessings, Divine Support, Otherworld, Sacrifice
Letter: Z
Deities: Valkyries, Heimdall, Freyja
Element: Air
Colors: White, Silver, Gold, Black, Rainbow
Animals: Elk, Swan, White Stag
Trees & Plants: Yew, Elk-Sedge
Oil: Peppermint
Crystals & Minerals: Amethyst, Clear Quartz

Swan maidens Algiz can mean "swan" and is connected with the divine flight of the Valkyries and swan maidens. Valkyries are divine protective beings who can fly and shape-shift into bird form. As "choosers of the slain," they carry the souls of the valiant dead to the appropriate afterlife in either Freyja's or Odin's halls. The method usually employed to enable flight is a magical feathered cloak called a *hamr*.

Swan maidens/Valkyries are the romantic protagonists in the poem *Völundarkviða*, from the *Poetic Edda*, where the elven Wayland the Smith and his two brothers meet and fall in love with three swan maidens. The partnerships went well for a few years until the swan maidens felt an undeniable migration urge and they left their men, flying away to fulfill their own fates. Swans are also linked to fate in *Snorri's Edda*, where it mentions that the first swans drank from the Norns' well, Urðarbrunnr. Another tale of a swan Valkyrie occurs in the legendary tale, *Hrómundar saga Gripssonar*, where a Valkyrie flies above the battle in swan form, casting spells in the hope of protecting her lover, Helgi. These stories exemplify the protective and liminal qualities of the Algiz rune.

Elk and elk-sedge An alternative name for this rune is Elhaz, meaning "elk" or "elk-sedge." The defensive quality of the elk's powerful antlers is deeply connected with this rune, as is the spiky elk-sedge plant that grows in fenlands.

The only poem we have for Algiz is the Anglo-Saxon rune poem, which speaks of the painful and bloody nature of the elk-sedge, and the dangers of grabbing it when walking in the fens. These are liminal places, which can be dangerous to wander into unprepared. Historically, fens were places where outlaws dwelled, or where the hunted could find sanctuary. Faeries and other liminal beings such as will-o'-the-wisps also dwell in fens and marshlands, and depending on our actions or intentions, they may choose to help or hinder our journeys.

Algiz's associations The shape of Algiz symbolizes open arms raised to the heavens, the shape of antlers, and the leaves of the sedge. It can represent the flight of birds, or perhaps their footprint. It also resembles a great tree with branches reaching up to the sky. Algiz can be worked with for journeying around Yggdrasil and therefore also relates to the god Heimdall, who guards and protects Bifröst, a bridge between the worlds. This rune is an opening to the heavens, a connection to the gods, and a call for divine aid. It is the Valkyries' feather cloak wrapped around us and the magic of soul flight. Algiz invokes the guidance of elk and the protection of his magnificent antlers. Although elk is the agreed antlered animal for Algiz, I often get the sense of a beautiful white stag when working with this rune, which connects with both the antlered and the otherworldly energies.

ALGIZ IN PRACTICE

Algiz helps us create necessary boundaries and allows us to find higher perspectives. We can work with Algiz when connecting with the gods, and when we embark upon a spiritual venture. As a rune of protection, it is gentler than Thurisaz and Eihwaz and so we can invoke Algiz when we wish for protection without confrontation. We experience Algiz when we feel the call of the otherworld, and the desire to journey with our guides and guardians.

Intoning Algiz is like an uplifting opening of the heart. It feels like a soul-deep safety and the wild knowledge of being at one with antler and feather.

Divination meanings

- Algiz can represent a need to call upon spiritual protection and guidance, or to know that you are being looked after.
- This rune denotes the blessings of the gods and a connection with the divine. It can be a sign that you are divinely guided and on the right path, and to trust your higher self and instincts.
- In conflict, Algiz advises the use of boundaries and barriers as a form of defense.

I rise to find you and drum you to sleep
I honor your dance, a warm spark I keep
Close to my heart on darkening days
I look for your light to show me the way

Sowilo (soh-will-oh)

This Ætt began with the hardships of hail and ice, and ends with the healing warmth of the sun. Now it is time to relax, celebrate, and bask in the light of Sowilo.

Keywords: Sun, Achievement, Healing, Direction, Creativity, Inner Purpose
Letter: S
Deities: Sól/Sunna, Baldr
Element: Fire
Colors: Orange, Yellow, Red
Animal: Eagle
Trees: Oak, Juniper
Oil: Juniper
Crystals & Minerals: Sunstone, Ruby

The warmth of Sowilo The literal meaning of Sowilo is "sun," and this rune represents all the shining, life-giving abundance of our home star. Sól, also known as Sunna, is the goddess connected with the sun and is a personification of solar power. As a rune of success and achievement, Sowilo acknowledges that while you may have traversed many challenges, you have come out the other side, both brighter and wiser.

Sowilo warms our bodies and brings light to our hearts. Although the sun is a vital, playful, and beneficial energy, Sowilo cautions against overexposure to her full power. If we stay in the strong sun for too long, we are likely to get burned, and if we stare directly at her, we can damage our eyes. The Icelandic rune poem mentions a shield named Svalinn that protects us from the extreme heat of the sun. As Sól makes her way across the sky, she holds up Svalinn to save the earth from burning under her rays.

Honoring the light The Old Norse poem celebrates the sun's light and speaks of bowing to holy judgment. This could possibly mean either bowing to the judgments of the gods or that people would have bowed to the sun to honor her light. In the creation myth (page 13), embers and sparks from the fires of Muspelheim were placed in the sky to create the sun, moon, and stars.

The poem *Völuspá*, from the *Poetic Edda*, says that at first all the celestial bodies did not know where they lived and lacked the rhythm of their cycles. Following life's bright rhythm is another important message from Sowilo. By allowing our bodies to move, to flow, and to dance, we often find our way through blocks and make breakthroughs. Dance brings the healing light of joy back into our lives and aligns us with the rhythm of our soul.

A rune of direction and healing The Anglo-Saxon rune poem expresses the importance of the sun for seafaring and navigation. Nowadays, it is hard to imagine how anyone could sail across vast oceans without any navigational equipment, but the Vikings journeyed to Iceland and discovered Greenland using only their knowledge of the sea, sun, and stars. It is likely that they used a simple sun compass, but of course, this relies on the sun making an appearance!

We can use Sowilo as a navigational tool to guide our own journey through life. If we feel emotionally or spiritually lost at sea, or that our spark has dimmed, Sowilo emerges like the sun through the clouds to lift us up and illuminate the way. Sowilo is a rune of healing, because the sun can relieve many ailments, including seasonal affective disorder. Ultraviolet light from the sun also helps our bodies produce vitamin D, which in turn supports our blood, bones, and immune system.

Sowilo helps us to find our direction and purpose

SOWILO IN PRACTICE

We know the sun is important to us, but how often do we pay real attention to her journey across the sky? If you are awake before sunrise, be sure to greet her first luminous rays piercing the dawn. And, when you are able to watch the sun set, take a moment to give thanks for the light of your day. Blessing the day not only honors our life-giving sun but also establishes a healthy awareness of the daily dance of light and life.

We can experience Sowilo through movement and dance, by finding the light on a dark day, and by allowing Sól's warm rays to heal us, body and soul.

Chanting Sowilo feels like a clearing of clouds to reveal the warmth and healing light of the sun. It is a smooth, clear, and heart-opening sound, and a reminder of the presence of joy.

Divination meanings

- Sowilo brings success, lasting achievements, and a bright hope for the future.
- It is a healing rune for mind, body, and soul.
- As a compass, Sowilo helps us to find our purpose and illuminates our true path.
- This rune brings a time of fertility, vitality, and joy. Harness this beautiful energy and move forward with confidence!

THE THIRD ÆTT

Týr's Ætt

The runes of the third and final Ætt are attributed to Týr, the one-handed Æsir god of justice, war, and honor. This Ætt explores themes of divinity, self-mastery, and a journey toward wholeness.

Týr's Ætt can be seen as an opportunity to integrate the lessons and experiences of the journey so far. It is a culmination of personal growth and encompasses concepts of divinity and social maturity. Týr is a fascinating character whose worship is undoubtedly old, and yet, compared with Odin and Thor, he is hardly mentioned in the Eddas. By studying Scandinavian place-names, it appears that Týr was much more popular in Denmark than in the rest of Scandinavia due to the high density of Týr-related place-names found there.

The main story that features Týr is the binding of the ferocious wolf, Fenrir, who was Loki's son. The Æsir gods feared the wolf because a seer had told them that he was destined to harm them. The gods bound Fenrir with strong ties but, growing bigger and stronger every day, the wolf was always able to break them. Týr was the only god who had the courage to approach and feed Fenrir, and so the wolf trusted him. The gods then presented Fenrir with a seemingly delicate, but unbreakable, magical binding. Suspicious of the gods' intentions, Fenrir refused to be tied with it unless one of the gods placed their hand in his mouth as an act of good faith. Týr was the only god to agree, and when Fenrir discovered he was unable to break the binding, he bit Týr's hand off. Týr sacrificed his sword hand and therefore lost his personal sovereignty in order to protect the wider community of the Æsir.

As an animal lover, this story always breaks my heart. Fenrir trusted Týr, and yet the god was honor bound to betray the wolf. I'm pretty sure this decision was exceptionally tough for Týr, who not only had bonded with Fenrir but also valued the truth of his word, along with the use of his hand!

This last Ætt invites us to contemplate the bigger picture and challenges us to consider the needs of the many versus the needs of the few.

Standing tall, heart to the sky
Faith is my arrow, Týr is my guide

Teiwaz (tey-warz)

Beginning the final Ætt with an arrow or spear pointing up to the heavens, Teiwaz is a bold symbol that guides us toward the correct course of action.

Keywords: Justice, Truth, Sacrifice, Star, Victory, Stability
Letter: T
Deity: Týr
Element: Air
Colors: Red, Yellow, Blue
Animals: Wolf, Eagle
Trees & Plants: Oak, Sage
Oils: Lemongrass, Lime
Crystals & Minerals: Carnelian, Coral, Lapis Lazuli

Týr's rune Although the rune shape for Teiwaz is clear, its meanings are more complex. This rune belongs to Týr, the one-handed god of victory and justice. Through learning the stories associated with Týr (page 70), we simultaneously learn about Teiwaz. Týr is a truly ancient deity and is thought to have once been a preeminent Germanic father-sky god. From this, Teiwaz can be seen as depicting a pillar holding up the celestial heavens, or a lightning bolt from above.

By the time the Eddas were written down, Týr's importance appears to have waned, with Odin and Thor taking on the roles of father and sky gods. However, in *Gylfaginning*, part of *Snorri's Edda*, Týr is described as a courageous god who decides who will be victorious in battle, and in *Sigrdrífumál*, part of the *Poetic Edda*, it is said that carving "victory runes" on to a sword hilt and invoking Týr twice will ensure success. It is likely that these victory runes were Teiwaz, because swords have been discovered with Teiwaz carved on to the hilt.

Teiwaz in the rune poems The Anglo-Saxon rune poem contains my favorite depiction of Teiwaz. It speaks of Týr as a guiding star that keeps its course and never fails. This evocative description connects with the strong and unwavering shape of the rune and resonates with Týr as a bright god of the heavens. The poem speaks of Týr's star guiding princes or nobles, and although this line could be referencing those of noble birth, the nature of this rune denotes noble action. I view this line as Teiwaz guiding all of us on an honorable path.

72 MEETING THE RUNES

The Old Norse poem focuses on Týr as the one-handed god. The second line mentions that Týr keeps the smiths busy, alluding to the rune's connection with the tools of war. Another interesting perspective is introduced in the Old Icelandic poem where, after referencing his wolf-devoured hand, Týr is called the temple's chief, which suggests he was also responsible for religious activities.

An honorable path From these sources, we can gather that Teiwaz has ancient and multifaceted meanings, but the thread that shines through is of taking the honorable course of action, having the courage to walk your soul's path, and being divinely guided from above. Through Týr's stories, we see him faced with situations that demand change and sacrifice. He moves from sky god to war god, from wolf-sitter to cultic leader. With each shift, he remains true to himself and expands majestically into each role.

TEIWAZ IN PRACTICE

Tuesday is named after Týr, so we invoke Týr at least once a week without realizing it! Tuesday is also considered to be ruled by Mars, which has led people to equate Týr with the Roman war god. I always find that Tuesday feels like a good day to take action, and so Týr can be called upon when we need to motivate ourselves to move forward in positive ways.

Týr and Teiwaz can be worked with in cases where we feel wronged and need to speak out about what we believe is right. On the other hand (no hand puns intended!), if we are dishonest, then Teiwaz calls us to take responsibility for these actions.

Chanting this rune sounds like a declaration of bright determination. The sound travels up and down my spine and I feel like my body takes on the shape of the rune. Intoning Teiwaz is an uplifting and grounding sound, simultaneously connecting us with the heavens and earth.

Divination meanings

- Teiwaz is a call for justice, law, and order, and reminds us to speak out, take action, and do the honorable thing.
- As a rune of stellar navigation, it can indicate that you are on the right track and that you have divine support.
- Týr knows sacrifice and loss and therefore Teiwaz can denote a time of powerful healing.

The light hidden within
The womb of the tomb
Opens the door once more

Berkano (ber-kah-no)

Meaning "birch goddess" or "birch tree," Berkano encompasses all aspects of the Earth Mother Goddess. It is a rune of the trees and whispers of feminine mysteries.

Keywords: Beginnings, Growth, Life Cycle, Nurturing, Purification, Shape-Shifter
Letter: B
Deities: Berchta/Perchta, Holda, Frigg, Urðr, Loki
Element: Earth
Colors: Green, Yellow, White
Animals: Bear, Hare
Tree: Birch
Oils: Geranium, Rose
Crystals & Minerals: Moonstone, Moss Agate

Birch trees Known as the "Lady of the Woods," birch is an elegant tree, whose silver-white bark brings light and grace to the forest. As a pioneer tree, it is quick to grow back after any disasters or deforestation. This repopulation links birch trees with concepts of rebirth and renewal. They are also connected with purification, and bundles of birch twigs have long been used in besoms to physically and energetically clear a space. A birch tree goddess who embodies the full life cycle is the Germanic goddess Berchta, also known as Perchta. Similar to Holda (pages 48–49), Berchta is a goddess of fertility who tends to the souls of dead children. She is a guardian of animals and is a shape-shifter who can take the form of a goose or swan. In winter, she can be seen flying across the sky with the Wild Hunt.

The cycles of life Berkano's shape is reminiscent of breasts, or of the breasts and stomach of a pregnant woman. This rune speaks of the cycles of life, birth, puberty, marriage, menopause, death, and renewal. The goddess of life is also the goddess of death, and the womb of the earth is also the tomb that holds us at the end of our days. In this respect, Berkano is a container; a hidden space of magic and transformation. As a giver of life, she is the Bright Mother, and as a keeper of the dead, she is the Dark Mother. These darker aspects are not to be feared but honored as necessary parts of wholeness.

Loki is a mischievous, trickster god, known for his shape-shifting abilities

Berkano in the rune poems The Old Norse rune poem contains an intriguing mention of the shape-shifting god, Loki. The poem begins by admiring the green-leafed birch and then mentions Loki as being lucky with deception. This could allude to the story where Loki shape-shifts into a mare to "distract" a giant's stallion in order to save the gods. Mare-Loki appears from the forest and lures the stallion back into the trees. Nine months later, Loki gives birth to Sleipnir, the eight-legged horse who becomes Odin's steed. Transformation among the trees, resulting in pregnancy and birth, is Berkano's magic in motion.

For me, birch trees have a faery-like quality, and people have often associated them with the otherworld. There are tales of people seeing faeries after falling asleep under a birch. The Old Icelandic poem brings an otherworldly quality to birch, mentioning the tree having leafy limbs, and continuing to talk about its spritely wood. The Anglo-Saxon poem challenges the fertility aspect of the birch, commenting on her lack of fruit, yet remarks that there is magic in her branches, and perhaps Berkano can be seen as supporting the process of birthing, more than symbolizing fertility itself.

BERKANO IN PRACTICE

Berkano is present at new beginnings, when we are starting afresh or launching a project. This rune is the tree of hope after a long winter and helps us to release the past and cleanse our space. We can connect with Berkano when we spend time with birch trees; perhaps we may get a glimpse of the birch goddess if we sit underneath her bower.

When we are moving into a new cycle of life, Berkano helps us to grieve what has been lost and prepares us for our next chapter. Shape-shifting is not just for changing physical form, but for allowing us to adapt to new situations. Berkano can help us with this magic. This rune reminds us that the goddess is all around us and supports us every step of the way.

Intoning Berkano is an enchanting sound, which can be intoned loudly or gently. Its energy connects with ancient mothers of the forest. You can also repetitively intone the first syllable, "ber," as a soothing, healing sound.

Divination meanings

- In a reading, Berkano can indicate new life awakening, birth, and fertility.
- It can also signify the presence of the divine feminine, entering a new phase of life, connecting with magical beings such as elves and faeries, and messages from the Mother Goddess.
- Berkano encourages self-care and nurturing healthy growth and creativity.

The night horses bring peace
Under restless hunters' skies

Ehwaz (eh-warz)

This is the rune of the horse and of partnership. On the surface, this may sound like a simple concept, but there are many aspects of journeying and partnership that can be explored with this rune.

Keywords: Horse, Partnership, Swiftness, Fertility, Mastery, Trust
Letter: E
Deities: Freyja, Freyr, Divine Twins, the Alcis, Hengist, Horsa, Sleipnir
Elements: Air, Earth
Colors: White, Green, Silver
Animal: Horse
Trees & Plants: Oak, Ash, Ragwort
Crystals & Minerals: Carnelian, Quartz, Optical Calcite

The shape of Ehwaz Visually, Ehwaz can be confusing because it looks like an "M" from the modern Latin alphabet. However, it represents the letter "E." The shape of Ehwaz can be seen as two horses' heads meeting in the center, or as two people holding hands. It can also be viewed as two Laguz runes (pages 82–84) reflecting each other. Ehwaz is a rune of flow and stability and opens the possibility of seeing yourself reflected in the other.

A rune of horses Before motors, horses were by far the swiftest and most comfortable way to travel across great distances of land. However, there is so much more to a partnership with an animal than we experience with a vehicle, and the connection between horse and rider has long been a sacred bond. I returned to horseback riding after a gap of more than twenty years, and in returning to ride as an adult, I learned a lot about honesty, boundaries, trust, communication, and the heart-healing connection that is possible between horse and human.

In Old Norse lore, a person could have a supernatural animal guardian called a *fylgja*, which was entwined with a person's family or represented an aspect of the soul. The companionship between horse and rider may have been seen to reflect this spiritual bond. Ehwaz can therefore represent the partnering of human and *fylgja*, or human and soul.

Odin's eight-legged steed Sleipnir is a magical horse who can travel swiftly throughout the nine worlds. The previous rune, Berkano (pages

Odin's steed, Sleipnir, is faster and more powerful than any other horse

74–76), was concerned with the conception and birth of Sleipnir, and it is perhaps no coincidence that Ehwaz is a rune associated with divine horses who are capable of otherworldly journeys.

Divine twins Ehwaz is connected with the divine twins, who are ancient horseback riding heroes or gods associated with Indo-European mythology. The Roman historian Tacitus spoke of divine twins called the Alcis and likened them to the Graeco-Roman twins Castor and Pollux. The Anglo-Saxon divine twins, named Hengist and Horsa, meaning "stallion" and "horse," were said to be descended from Odin. Freyja and Freyr (page 24) are divine twins of the Vanir gods, who are intrinsically linked with the fertility of the land. Horses are sacred to both of them, and Freyr received them as offerings and kept them at his sanctuary in northern Norway.

Ehwaz in the rune poems It is only the Anglo-Saxon rune poem that mentions Ehwaz, and it speaks of horses being a princely joy, connected with nobility. It also mentions that horses bring comfort to the restless. Horses were a matter of pride for the nobility and helped them to ride in to or away from battles. The idea of Ehwaz bringing comfort to the restless suggests that this rune supports forward motion, travel, and adventures. These adventures could be physical, but they could also be of a spiritual nature. Ehwaz can represent riding between the worlds upon the branches of Yggdrasil. In this sense, it is a rune connected with the magical practice of *seiðr*, a type of trance prophecy that Freyja taught to Odin.

EHWAZ IN PRACTICE

We experience Ehwaz when building trusting and harmonious partnerships. Although Ehwaz is exalted in loving marriages, it is also a rune of deep friendships and soulmate connections with your pets. And, of course, Ehwaz is always present when we make friends with a horse.

Ehwaz could be calling when we feel restless and wish to explore new opportunities. We are working with the rune's energies when taking big leaps forward in our lives. Within spiritual work, we meet Ehwaz when we look inward and get to know all aspects of ourselves. Ehwaz is the rune of the witch or the shaman who journeys through the worlds.

Chanting Ehwaz is like calling for a horse across the plains. It is the summoning of spirit, and an opening to the road ahead. Conversely, in ritual, you may like to whisper or quietly chant Ehwaz as you open the ways between the worlds.

Divination meanings

- In a reading, Ehwaz represents union and harmony. It is a sign of positive relationships and the possibility of marriage and fertility.
- Ehwaz means things could be moving forward swiftly now, and that you are ready to broaden your horizons and take a leap of faith.
- It is a rune of spiritual progress and a deep connection with your guides.
- Ehwaz is a sign to trust the path you are on and to know that the desired changes are imminent.

The sky is open and I am calling
I hear the ravens cry
To the Father of Knowing

Mannaz (man-arz)

The meaning of Mannaz is "mankind." It represents all of humanity and embodies the mysteries of being human.

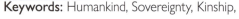

Keywords: Humankind, Sovereignty, Kinship, Power, Intelligence, Divine Structure
Letter: M
Deities: Odin, Frigg, Heimdall
Element: Air
Colors: Deep Red, Purple, Blue, Orange
Animals: Raven, Hawk
Tree: Holly
Crystals & Minerals: Garnet, Red Tiger's Eye

The human experience Mannaz is the marriage between the Sky Father and the Earth Mother and the connection between human and divine. It is a rune of maturity and intelligence and it represents a more nuanced understanding of the human experience, and an acknowledgment of the divine light that dwells within each person. The shape of Mannaz is two Wunjo runes (pages 44–45) facing each other, and it contains the Gebo rune (pages 42–43) at its center. Mannaz holds deeper meanings of these previous runes.

If Wunjo is the pleasure of a partner and Gebo is the promise, then Mannaz is the marriage.

Mannaz's association with Odin Mannaz is related to Odin and in particular to his ravens, Huginn and Muninn. Odin sends his ravens to fly out through the worlds every day, collecting numinous wisdom. The poem *Grímnismál*, from the *Poetic Edda*, recounts how Odin frets that they may not return. Odin and his wife Frigg are the sovereign powers of the Æsir gods, and their union represents the essence of Mannaz. If we see the points of Mannaz as being beaks, we can visualize this rune as two ravens returning to Odin as he sits upon his throne.

Mannaz in the source texts The fullness of the life cycle is referenced in the Anglo-Saxon rune poem. The verse begins with celebrating the joy of kinship but continues by stating that all men betray each other in the end when our bodies return to the earth. As Wunjo is a celebration of joy, the double Wunjo of Mannaz represents the

80 MEETING THE RUNES

bittersweet understanding that all we love must eventually pass. However, this knowledge hopefully allows us to appreciate our blessings even more.

The Old Norse poem speaks of men being created from earth, and hints that hawks hold power over us. Hawks and birds of prey have powerful links to death and rebirth in the mythological poems. Freyja owns a feathered cloak called a *válshamr*, which transforms the wearer into a falcon. When Iðunn, the goddess of immortality, is kidnapped by the *jötunn* Thjazi, Loki borrows Freyja's cloak and flies off to rescue the goddess. Without Iðunn, the gods began to age and lose vigor, but the falcon returns the goddess, thus saving the gods from certain death. This myth suggests that although we are made of earth and will return to it, the hawk rescues the part of us that is immortal.

Heimdall relates to Mannaz because of his role in creating the structures of society as described in the poem *Rigsþula*. Power and structure are important aspects of Mannaz. However, the true power of this rune is to implement structures that support the community, not oppress it.

MANNAZ IN PRACTICE

Mannaz is the rune of the sovereign self. We experience it when we speak and act from a place of integrity. It is a rune that helps us when working with others or when considering our role within the broader community.

As a rune of self-awareness, we can work with Mannaz when we wish to commune with the different aspects of the soul. When connecting with Mannaz, I like to imagine Huginn and Muninn are sitting upon my shoulders, whispering secrets into my ears.

Chanting Mannaz is a clear, strong, and rooted sound. It calls out to connect with others.

Divination meanings

- In a reading, the appearance of Mannaz can indicate a time of success and stepping into personal power. It denotes the importance of staying true to yourself and your values.
- Mannaz represents the power that we use for something greater than our own personal gain and helps us to create healthy structures.
- It is a rune that signifies divine connections and indicates a powerful time on your spiritual path.
- Mannaz can also represent an initiation, or rite of passage.
- As a rune of friendship, it denotes the opportunity to celebrate with and honor your kith and kin.

I am caught under waves
A bubbling cauldron arises in me
Deep diving mirrors
Weeping sea glass

Laguz (lar-gooz)

As a rune of water, Laguz encompasses all expanses and experiences of the element. It is a rune of the unfathomable oceans, mountainous waterfalls, still lakes, and dancing streams.

Keywords: Water, Emotions, Flow, Expansion, Wyrd, Healing
Letter: L
Deities: Njörðr, Rán, Ægir, Frigg
Element: Water
Colors: Blue, Green
Animals: Sea Serpent, Seal, Fish, Seabirds
Tree: Willow
Oil: Jasmine
Crystals & Minerals: Pearl, Amber, Aquamarine

Seafaring For our ancestors, water was not only a necessity for survival but also represented a chance for expansion and adventure. The Vikings are remembered for their great feats of seamanship, yet these journeys came at a great risk as waves swallowed up countless Viking ships.

The sea goddess Rán and her husband Ægir rule over the oceans with their nine daughters, who personify the waves. Rán embodies the crueler aspects of the ocean as she takes the drowned seafarers to dwell in her watery realm.

The Vanir god Njörðr is seen as a more amiable lord of the waters and is called upon to aid those who travel upon the seas. He is particularly a friend of fishermen.

Laguz in the rune poems The opportunities and inherent dangers of seafaring are the focus of the Anglo-Saxon rune poem, where a ship is called a sea stallion that can't always be controlled.

The force of water and waterfalls is mentioned in the Old Norse rune poem, followed by an intriguing mention of gold being costly. We could see this as regarding trade and gold being carried across waters, or this could reference Ægir's gold, which is mentioned in *Skáldskaparmál*, from Snorri's *Edda*. When Ægir entertains the gods with a feast, he uses gold, instead of fire, to illuminate his oceanic halls. The Icelandic poem speaks of the different powers of water, from an eddying stream to a gushing geyser. The circular motion of eddying water could allude to the source of life or of returning to that primal source.

Laguz is a symbol of flow and change

The deities associated with Laguz This rune flows through the three sacred wells of Yggdrasil (page 15) and is intrinsically linked with concepts of fate and wisdom. The Norns' well, Urðarbrunnr, holds the waters of *wyrd*, or fate; Mímisbrunnr is Mímir's spring of wisdom; and Hvergelmir, called the bubbling cauldron, is the primal source of all rivers. Laguz is linked with the waters of *wyrd*, but also with weaving fate and spinning magic. The goddess Frigg has a magical distaff, which can shape the threads of *wyrd*.

Bodies of water are sacred, liminal spaces and have long been seen as places to connect with gods and spirits. Since the Neolithic period, people have given votive offerings to the water. Weapons and jewelry in vast numbers were discovered in Denmark's Lake Tissø, which were likely an offering to Týr, as the lake is named after him.

The shape of Laguz This rune can be seen as a wave, a seahorse's head, a sea serpent arching above the waves, the prow of a ship, or a distaff. Interestingly, leeks are also connected with Laguz. According to the *Völuspá*, part of the *Poetic Edda*, they were the first vegetable to grow when the worlds were being formed, and were considered a sign of purification and fertility.

LAGUZ IN PRACTICE

Water is all around and within us. We are born into the world through water, and, in many mythologies, we leave this life by crossing a river to the realm of the dead.

Laguz connects with healing wells, natural springs, and deep subterranean rivers. More than half of our bodies comprise of water, and so this rune also governs the tides within us. We can experience Laguz by visiting and meditating with different bodies of water. Feeling the weightlessness of swimming and the power of a waterfall helps us to receive Laguz's healing. If possible, collect water from a natural spring and bless it by chanting Laguz over it.

As a rune of the dreamworld, we can connect with Laguz by recording the messages that come through in our dreams. Laguz is also a muse for musicians and poets who often work with water as a metaphor to encapsulate the mysteries of the heart, soul, and the otherworld.

Chanting Laguz creates a cleansing energy that helps us to clear and bless a space and calm our minds. It feels like water flowing through us as we chant.

Divination meanings

- When Laguz appears in a reading, it is often a sign to listen to our emotions, our intuition, and our dreams.
- It can indicate a time of fertility or deep healing.
- Laguz brings cleansing to situations and opens up the horizons for new opportunities and adventures.

*Light the dawn and stir my heart
Awaken now the frozen dark*

Inguz (ing-ooz)

This is the rune of the seed and of the divine gateway. Like a seed, Inguz may appear simple on the outside, but it holds deep magic safe within its core.

Keywords: Seed, Fertility, Potential, Gateway, Ancestor, Earth, Growth
Letter (Sound): Ng
Deities: Freyr, Ing, Nerthus
Element: Earth
Colors: Green, Yellow, Orange, Gold, Brown
Animals: Boar, Stag, Horse, Cow
Tree: Apple
Crystals & Minerals: Amber, Peridot, Moss Agate

The deities connected with Inguz Also called Ingwaz (ing-warz), Inguz is a rune of masculine fertility and relates to the Germanic ancestral deity named Ing or Ingvi. Only the Anglo-Saxon rune poem speaks of Inguz and it mentions Ing as being a hero and a divine progenitor among the East Danes. He is said to go over the waves to the east riding in his chariot.

Ing likely predates the Old Norse Yngvi, who ultimately became amalgamated with Freyr and was known as Yngvi-Freyr. He ensured the fertility of the land and of the individual, and is associated with abundance and pleasure, with his statues often displaying his erect phallus.

Fertility rituals Chariots were cultic vehicles, and chariots carrying statues of the virile Freyr were carried around fields to encourage crop fertilization. Festivities in honor of the earth goddess Nerthus also included a processional chariot and one such festival was recorded by the Roman historian Tacitus—a priest would accompany a chariot carrying the goddess through the settlements. This procession involved great festivities where peace reigned, and iron weapons were put away. At the end of the festival, the chariot and the goddess were cleansed in a sacred lake, with the last part of the ritual involving a sacrifice to recharge the goddess's energy. These chariot rituals endured for millennia and involved both fertility gods and goddesses.

The Inguz rune is connected with this ancient ritual spreading of fertility, and the shape of the rune is reminiscent of both male and female sexual organs. We can also see Kenaz (pages 39–41) and Jera (pages 56–58) in the Inguz rune. As well as the diamond shape, Inguz has another form—two "X" shapes stacked on top of each other. This form has an uncanny resemblance to DNA.

A divine gateway Freyr dwells in Álfheimr, the home of the light elves, and he is deeply connected with the wild spirits of the land. Inguz can be worked with as a gateway between the worlds, particularly to the realm of faeries. As people have moved away from nature and a belief in nature spirits, the portals between the worlds are thought to have closed. However, working with Inguz alongside the nature spirits help us to reopen the ways.

Hidden potential Seeds contain all the potential for their growth and fulfillment within their unassuming form and need to be planted deep within the earth to gestate and gain strength. This is an important lesson of the Inguz rune. Every creative process needs to be protected through its most vulnerable phase, so it has the best chance of powerfully manifesting in the world.

Inguz represents the need to nourish and protect your seedling plans

INGUZ IN PRACTICE

Experiencing Inguz is experiencing the cycles of nature and getting to know the land we love, or getting to love the land we know. As I'm writing this, we are approaching the pagan festival of Imbolc. Celebrated in early February, it marks the beginning of spring, and is when the seed spark of life deep in the earth is keenly felt. Inguz encourages participation in the life cycle. Depending on the time of year, you can work with Inguz by planting seeds while focusing on your hopes and wishes, taking time out to enjoy the spring and summer flowers, and harvesting fruits and giving thanks for your blessings. Remember to share a little of your harvest with the spirits of the land.

There are a variety of ways you can intone Inguz. Because the sound it represents is "ng," you can chant "ing," which has the feeling of something growing deep in the earth. Or, you can chant the full name as either "ing-ooz" or "ing-warz," and these sounds can be felt as a warm feeling in your tummy, or as energy rising in your body.

Divination meanings

- Inguz signals a time to celebrate the abundance of life.
- It represents potential being manifested. Inguz appears when we are doing amazing inner work, which will manifest as success when the time is right.
- Inguz can represent a period of gestation, so its appearance in a reading may indicate a quiet time of rest. Sometimes the light of progress and success can occur only when we allow ourselves the deep dark space to evolve.
- As a rune of fertility, Inguz symbolizes abundance and stability in love and career readings.
- It signifies attraction between people, and is a rune that boosts our vitality.

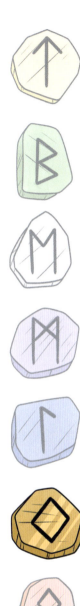

Sacred and wild memories of stone
Roots digging deep through flesh and bone

Othala (oh-tha-la)

This rune represents home and belonging, which can be a sense of belonging to our clan or to the land.

Keywords: Homeland, Ancestors, Identity, Prosperity, Legacy, Tradition
Letter: O
Deity: Odin
Elements: Earth, Fire
Colors: Red, Yellow, Orange
Animals: Personal or Familial Animal Guides
Tree: Hawthorn
Crystals & Minerals: Black Obsidian, Petrified Wood, Smoky Quartz

A rune of legacy If Inguz (pages 85–87) represents the wholeness of the fertile land, then Othala is the roots we put down and the homestead we build. It is a rune of legacy that helps us to contemplate what we wish to offer the following generations. Othala is an ancestral song humming through our veins and the knowing in our bones. We see Othala in the rings of an old tree and in the spirals of our fingerprints. It is a rune that remembers those who are no longer with us and the stories we tell about them.

Attitudes toward home and legacy are probably very different to how they were one hundred years ago, let alone in the Viking Age. We are very lucky to be living in an age that offers us opportunities for comfort, work, and connection that would not have been possible for our ancestors. Our "clan" could live on the opposite side of the world and yet, thanks to technology, we are able to connect with them in an instant. However, our departure from nature and community has left many of us lacking a sense of belonging. This is perhaps partly why people feel drawn to connecting with the runes and other pagan or nature-based practices, because it feels like a homecoming for the soul.

Othala in the rune poems The Anglo-Saxon rune poem is the only source for Othala, and it mentions the joys of family prosperity alongside the desire to enjoy the security of home. The poem goes on to speak of privilege, which is, quite rightly, a problematic word, but in the case of Othala, I see it linked to honorable behavior. As a rune of honor, hospitality, and reciprocity, Othala asks us to think about the consequences of our actions and the kind of world we wish to create.

Seek guidance and insight from the ancestors by practicing *útiseta*

Ancestral wisdom Connecting with the ancestors was important for most pre-Christian cultures, with people visiting burial sites and mounds to receive ancestral guidance and support. Some Old Norse sorcerers practiced *útiseta* ("sitting out"), which is a magical technique used to gain wisdom or power from the ancestors of the land by literally sitting out in nature at potent times. Honoring the ancestors is a vital part of the Othala rune, however this can bring up some painful issues for us. Not all of our ancestors were good or wise, and many of us are disconnected from our families. What I have learned from this work is that there are circles of ancestors who support us, even if they are not our direct family, and working with Othala can heal some of these wounds.

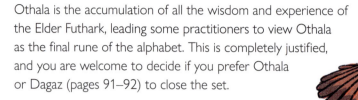

Othala is the accumulation of all the wisdom and experience of the Elder Futhark, leading some practitioners to view Othala as the final rune of the alphabet. This is completely justified, and you are welcome to decide if you prefer Othala or Dagaz (pages 91–92) to close the set.

OTHALA IN PRACTICE

We experience Othala with those people and places that make us feel like home. Othala is a fire in our hearts when we feel loved, safe, and secure. It teaches us the path of finding safety, love, and belonging within ourselves. We can experience Othala at family celebrations (chosen or blood family) and by remembering those who have passed. If it is accessible, visiting burial mounds, cairns, and sacred sites helps us to connect with the ancestors. Exploring your family tree can be a healing and helpful way to connect with Othala.

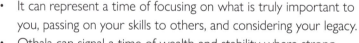
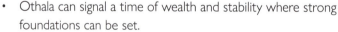

As a rune of legacy and of the land, Othala encourages us to tend to environmental issues, big or small. By picking up litter on our walks, planting trees, or supporting wildlife groups, we can all do our bit to safeguard our sacred land.

Intoning Othala reminds us that we are home within ourselves. It is a feeling of deep roots and new leaves, and it invokes the memories of people and places we love.

Divination meanings

- Othala can mean the joys of belonging, feeling accepted, and loved. This might be in the form of feeling a sacred connection with the land, feeling "at home" within yourself, or connecting with the ancestors.
- It can represent a time of focusing on what is truly important to you, passing on your skills to others, and considering your legacy.
- Othala can signal a time of wealth and stability where strong foundations can be set.

*For I thread light for you, galaxies spin me in two
I spiral light upon your face, a gift divine of love and grace*

Dagaz (day-garz)

Meaning "day," Dagaz is a rune of light and transcendence. It is the meeting point between past and present and the moment of calm between storms.

Keywords: Day, Transformation, Awakening, Ending/Beginning, Gateway, Hope
Letter: D
Deities: Dagr, Nótt
Elements: Fire, Air
Colors: Red, Yellow, Orange, Blue
Animals: Dragonfly, Butterfly, Hawk
Trees: Rowan, Spruce
Oil: Clary Sage
Crystals & Minerals: Peridot, Emerald, Clear Quartz, Citrine, Sunstone

The twenty-fourth rune As the final rune of the Elder Futhark, Dagaz represents endings and beginnings. It is a rune of flowing energy; a never-ending figure of eight, continually birthing the next moment. Although it is debatable whether Dagaz or Othala (pages 88–90) is the final rune, I like to work with Dagaz because its cyclical nature circles us back to the beginning. As one rune journey ends, Dagaz opens the door to Fehu (pages 26–27) once more.

Night and day Dagaz embodies two phrases: "the dark night of the soul" and "it's always darkest before the dawn." As the dark night, Dagaz represents spiritual trials and initiation, and speaks of those times when we just can't see the light. The hour before dawn is the darkest and coldest part of night—just like a problem feels at its worst before resolutions come. As daylight illuminates a cold dark sky, Dagaz is the healing blessing after hardship. The rune can represent the liminal times of dawn and dusk.

We witness an extremely long, dark night of the soul in the poem *Sigrdrífumál*, from the *Poetic Edda*, where the Valkyrie Sigrdrífa had been under a sleep spell for many years. On waking, her first act is to ritually "hail" the day and ask for victory. This joyful greeting of the daylight, with the hope of better times, is the essence of Dagaz.

Dagaz in the rune poems Dagaz is undoubtedly an ancient symbol, with its likeness carved into stones from the Neolithic period. However, it is only the Anglo-Saxon rune poem that mentions this rune. It speaks of the day being dear to all, whether people are rich or poor, and states that day is the herald of the lord, suggesting that Dagaz is a messenger of light. The poem also mentions the light of the great judge, which could relate to a period of spiritual realization and transformation.

Endings and beginnings Each rune is a gateway for us to journey through, but Dagaz represents a gateway between life stages. It can be a rune of birthing and bringing new life into the world, or it can suggest that a phase of life is over and we are about to embark upon our next adventure. As a rune of initiations and of journeying into the unknown, Dagaz requires inner strength. It is the rune of the seeker, the witch, the shaman, and all those who quest for divine truths.

DAGAZ IN PRACTICE

Although concepts of this rune can be logically grasped, Dagaz seeks to be experienced. Dagaz moments can be found if we rise to greet the morning sun, or when watching the last rays sink behind the clouds. We can feel Dagaz in the magical extremes of the solstices, or in the moments of balance within the equinoxes. Dagaz is the butterfly emerging from the cocoon and the dragonfly darting into our vision.

Chanting Dagaz is bright, joyful, and vibrates in the solar plexus and the heart. It is a celebration of light and the feeling of achievement. We can intone Dagaz at dawn to greet the day, and in the evening to give thanks for the light.

Divination meanings

- Dagaz appears when we are in the midst of transformation and is the breakthrough we are seeking. It is the sign of a new dawn and represents a turning point, and hope for the future.
- This rune illuminates the possibility of positive change. It is a sign that one cycle is over, and to take a breath before the next adventure begins.
- Dagaz is peace after hardship and light after dark.
- It is a sign that you have accomplished much and that new opportunities are coming your way.
- It represents a time of renewal and encourages us to take a leap of faith.

The blank rune

Also known as the *wyrd* rune, or Odin's rune, the blank rune is quite a controversial topic among rune readers.

Keywords: Unknowable, Wyrd, Fate, Mystery

The blank rune is a modern invention and there is historically no mention of it before the 1980s. However, since it is regularly included in purchased rune sets, it is worth discussing, allowing you to choose whether you wish to include this twenty-fifth rune in your rune work or not. Personally, I do not work with the blank rune because, although it has some fascinating aspects, it essentially embodies very similar meanings as Perthro (page 61–63). I do, however, know some wonderful rune experts who like to include it in their work.

The blank rune is said to represent *wyrd*, fate, and the unknowable. Its emptiness is the mystery of the gods and pure, unmanifested potential. We could see it as Odin's sacrificed eye, the one that we do not outwardly see but know exists deep within the god Mímir's well. Odin sacrificed one eye for a drink from Mímir's well of wisdom, and this drink allowed him to become the wisest of all gods. We could also see the blank rune as the Norns' well, a place of deep memory and ever-unfolding futures. It is a space between the worlds, a moment in between our inhale and exhale.

THE BLANK RUNE IN PRACTICE

As guidance, this rune counsels silence. When the blank rune appears, know that there is nothing to do at this time. It is a rune of patience, and of understanding that the gods may not always reply, but they do listen. It may represent the need to wait until we see the bigger picture before we take action, or it could suggest that events are already unfolding behind the scenes, which we are currently not permitted to see. It is a rune of unexpected events, but it could also indicate that deep down, you already know the answer you seek. In a fast-moving world of ready information, this rune allows space for silence and surrender.

If we work with the blank rune, we are asked to open up to the unknowable, to listen for whispers on the wind, and to allow for life's tapestry to unfold without us tampering with it.

CHAPTER

Divination with the runes

Now that we have connected with the runes and learned about their energies, we are ready to begin our own magical journey with them. There are many different ways we can work with runes. In this chapter, we explore divination, which is the most commonly known modern use of runes.

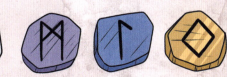

The history of runic divination

Divination is the esoteric art of discovering something that was previously hidden. People have been using runes for divination for thousands of years.

Historically, divination was employed for foretelling the future, problem-solving, seeking direction, or looking to alter one's fate, but the word is also associated with deities, the divine, and of being in communion with the shining heavens. This is part of the beauty of the runes—they allow us to reach out to the gods and guides and receive reflections, revelations, and guidance for our lives.

Perhaps the first recorded account we have of runic divination is from the Roman historian Tacitus in around 98 CE. Tacitus stated that Germanic people held divination in high regard and that, to decide on a course of action, rune-like symbols were inscribed on to strips of wood, which were then thrown, or cast (page 112), on to a white cloth. Odin also established the importance of rune casting in the poem *Hávamál*, from the *Poetic Edda*, in which he tests the reader's knowledge of runic divination, asking, "Do you know how to cast?"

Although we would love our knowledge of runic divination to be inherited from an unbroken lineage from the distant past, unfortunately this is just not the case because very few pagan or pre-Christian spiritual practices have been passed down through the ages. Various divination systems have been channeled and created over the last millennia, and in the 1980s the modern system of divining with runes became popular through a range of books and rune kits.

However, there are a couple of things I'd like to say to anyone feeling disappointed with the lack of evidence for historical rune casting. Firstly, people have always looked for answers, signs, and meanings in life and sought out ways of communing with gods and guides via divination and oracles. Although we live in very different times today, our needs, worries, and desires are essentially the same as those of our ancestors. We all want health, safety, abundance, and to love and be loved.

All symbols and languages evolve over time, and their meanings can be portrayed in different lights depending on the social, cultural, and political climate. It is therefore natural that the runes have also evolved, and their meanings have expanded to encompass our modern issues. Although runes can adapt to our modern lives, they also have the power to call us back to our primal and elemental selves and remind us of our inherent connection to the land.

Secondly, each rune is a gateway we can journey through. When we actively engage with the runes, they show us who and what they are, and their energies are very much their own, unspoiled by the passing of time. As we quest to respectfully understand them, and ourselves, we gain access to ancient pools of wisdom and inspiration that encourage us to embark upon our own runic journeys, just as our ancestors did before us.

The runes can reveal the swirling energies that are within and around us, and can help us to find the necessary calmness, clarity, and understanding. They can help us to understand our present situations and reveal the deeper themes and what powers are at play. They show which paths lead to healing, and which appear to bring further challenges. They can help us to understand our life path and the threads and patterns of our days.

Getting started

There are a few things you might wish to have close by before you begin your work with the runes.

YOUR RUNES

Firstly, and most importantly, of course, is a rune set! There are plenty of gorgeous sets you can purchase in shops and online, and I do happily own and work with a few. However, it is the ones I made myself that always hold the most personal magic. I explain how to create your own magical runes on pages 116–120.

A RUNE BAG OR BOX

The container in which you keep your runes is also an object of power. If we look after our runes, they will look after us, and so it is wise to keep your runes in a nice bag or box, which you could buy, or you could make yourself. It can be as plain or as ornate as you wish. The most important thing is that it feels sacred and joyful to you. Your choice of container will also depend on what you intend to do with the set. For example, I have a rune set on my altar for personal divination work, which I keep in a decorated box, whereas I have a strong cotton pouch for the runes that I like to take outside and work with on the land.

A RUNE CLOTH

A rune cloth is a piece of material that is used to place or cast runes on to for divination. It is not essential to work with a rune cloth, particularly when you are getting started, but you may wish to use one when you are further along your journey. Although Tacitus recorded that rune cloths were traditionally white, there are plenty of beautifully decorated cloths available if you prefer something more colorful, or you could always repurpose material that you already own. If you are feeling creative, you may wish to experiment with fabric pens and paints to create your own decorated rune cloth—perhaps inscribe the runes around the edge of the cloth, or draw or trace Yggdrasil, one of the gods, the Norns, a dragon, or other magical being on to the cloth.

You could also create an elemental cloth by splitting the cloth into four equal parts, with a section for earth, air, fire, and water. In each segment, draw symbols, swirls, or images that represent the element. Elemental (or other specific) cloth designs can give structure to readings—an example is given in the elemental rune spread on page 110.

A MAGICAL NOTEBOOK

Dedicating a notebook to recording your runic journey is an important and special part of the work. Your runic notebook is a place where your wisdom will expand and develop over time, and it will be a faithful companion on your journey, which you can reflect upon to remember your wild adventures between the worlds.

I am a huge fan of handwritten journals, because there is something deeply therapeutic about expressing yourself with pen, pencil, and paint on paper. Another idea is to cut out images and words from magazines to create a collage about each rune. You can, of course, create digital journals if this is your preferred method of note-keeping. This does make it easier if you want to change your work later!

Tips for your rune notebook

- Allow generous sections in your book for each rune to give you the space to note down all the meanings and correspondences that speak to you.
- Journal your experiences, readings, and meditations with the different runes.
- Read the rune poems and note your responses to these source texts. Which verses or lines do you connect with? Which ones feel odd to you?
- Read the work of different rune experts and take on board the insights that feel right to you. Over time, as your knowledge grows, you will develop your own correspondences and personal language with the runes.

How to approach readings

What I love about reading runes is that they can help unravel the mysteries of our daily lives and remind us of the opportunities and power available to us.

When we look at other divination systems, like tarot or oracle cards, although it is hugely beneficial to understand the cards' meanings, you can glean a fair amount of information from intuitively reading the often beautiful images on the cards. With the runes, it is a little more complex, because essentially you are looking at simple lines. This is the brilliance of runes—these lines are symbolic gateways that open up to rich wisdom and guidance, but when you are learning, sometimes they can *just* look like lines! You can refer back to Chapter 2 where I offer divination meanings for each rune.

The most important thing about approaching the runes for divination is that we calm and still our minds and take a few moments to center ourselves before asking any questions. In today's world, we often run around so fast, with our brains processing countless stimuli and information, that it can be hard to find the space to listen for what we truly feel. The meditations on pages 101–103 allow stillness and connection, and you can use them before you start a reading, healing, ritual, or spell work. Once we have centered our energy, it is easier to understand how we are feeling and what is driving our questions.

ASKING THE "RIGHT" QUESTIONS

Runes offer grounded and honest reflections of our lives and reveal threads of our destiny. Will they answer specific, detailed questions? Maybe, but possibly not with the exact details we might require.

When I talk about asking the "right" questions, it isn't a judgment or a test, but more of an opportunity to get the most out of a reading. My experience has been that by asking questions such as "Will … happen to me?" or "Should I …?", we throw away our power and receive diluted readings from whichever divination tool we are using. By approaching the runes with questions like "Which path would best support my growth and healing?", "How can I make the most of this opportunity?", or "What do I need to know about …?" we retain agency and will therefore receive more coherent, empowering readings.

Topics you could ask about include the energy of places, houses, jobs, or social situations, and how to navigate change. Love and relationships are often the driving force behind divination questions and, although we might not ask the runes about "tall dark strangers," we could ask about what is required to encourage greater love in our lives.

MEDITATION: CALMING AND GROUNDING

You can practice this meditation before beginning a rune reading, or when you simply need a quick method of calming and grounding yourself.

1. Sit in a comfortable position, with your back as straight as possible.
2. Place one hand on your tummy and the other over your heart.
3. Close your eyes and gently take some deep breaths. Become aware of the simple rise and fall of your chest as you breathe.
4. Listen to the sound of your breath—breathe in and breathe out. Allow your hands to rest by your side if you wish.
5. Now begin to count your breath and hold on the inhale and exhale. Inhale for the count of four and hold for the count of four; exhale for the count of four and hold for the count of four.
6. Repeat this as many times as you need until you feel a sense of calm.
7. When you are ready, open your eyes and notice how you feel calmer and clearer.

HOW TO APPROACH READINGS **101**

MEDITATION: CONNECTING TO ROOTS AND STAR

If you would like to continue deeper into a meditative space, you can follow the previous meditation with this mini journey to connect with your personal roots and star.

1. Sit comfortably with your eyes closed and allow your breathing to be deep and rhythmical.
2. Follow the flow of your breath throughout your body. Feel your inhale as a wave of life-force energy flowing through your body, from your head down to your toes. Feel your exhale as a release of everything that no longer serves you, and everything you want to let go. Release it with gratitude on your exhale.
3. From where you are seated, visualize or feel roots coming out from your feet or the base of your spine. These are your own personal roots that connect you to the earth. These roots could be any color and any texture—they are your roots and reflect your energy at this time.
4. On each exhale, feel these roots digging deeper into the earth. They dig through soil, rock, and bone. They dig through the layers of mantle, down toward the molten core of the earth.
5. Now, on your inhale, feel your roots drinking up golden life-force energy from the earth's core. Feel that light flowing up through your roots, up through your feet, and into your body. Each breath fills your body with energy from the earth, until you are filled with golden light.
6. From the top of your head, feel a thread of light flowing through your crown and out, up into the sky. Up the thread of light goes through blue, through indigo, and up into darkness, where your thread is seeking your own personal star. With ease, you find your north star, and the thread reaches up to it, allowing starlight to flow down the thread into your body.
7. Now, on each breath, feel guiding light from your star filling you with silver light, and the energy from the earth filling you with golden light. Allow these energies to mix in your body as you feel a radiant connection with the deep earth and the shining heavens.

From this connected and energized space, you are ready to take on the nine worlds! Or at the very least, ready to conduct divination or magical workings. When you have finished, remember to "close down" this connection following the steps opposite.

102 DIVINATION WITH THE RUNES

1. Starting with the heavens, gently disconnect the thread from your star and sense the thread coming down through the blue sky to your crown, where it returns into the top of your head.
2. Feel the crown of your head firmly "shut." Then, disconnect your roots from the earth's core and allow your roots to climb up through all the layers of earth, stone, and bone until they rest, perhaps, just beneath your feet.

I always like to keep my roots just touching the land, but the choice is yours. If you feel you have too much energy, the earth will always be grateful for us to return any extra energy back to the land.

Methods of runic divination

There are different ways of using the runes for divination. They can be laid out in particular patterns, called spreads, or "cast" by throwing them down.

CHOOSING YOUR RUNES

You can select your runes either by picking them directly out of your rune bag or box, or by laying them out face down on a cloth and choosing the runes that call to you. Close your eyes, hover your hands over the runes, and feel if you are drawn to any in particular. This could be a warm or cold sensation in your hands, or you might be drawn in a certain direction over the set.

RUNE SPREADS

Any number of runes can be used in a rune spread, from a single rune to the full set of twenty-four (or twenty-five in some sets—see page 93). Spreads can help you to find answers to specific questions, or gain insight about a situation or your life in general. Here are some rune spreads you might like to try for inspiration.

Rune for the day spread

A simple, one-rune spread is a great way to learn the runes and incorporate them into your daily life. Relax your mind, focus your attention on the day, and feel the rune that is calling to you. Refer to the information about your chosen rune in Chapter 2 and allow the stories and meanings of the rune to flow through you.

- Look at the rune's correspondences and see if you can incorporate its associated colors, crystals, or oils into your day.
- Intone or chant the rune and draw it in your journal or place it on your altar.
- If you enjoy research, look into the stories of the gods and other beings connected with the rune and journal your discoveries.

Varying the time of day for your reading can bring different results. Morning readings are great for setting up the energy and focus for your day, whereas evening readings can be gentle opportunities to reflect on the day's events and experiences.

Sól & Máni's spread

This two-rune spread focuses on your inner and outer realities. In Old Norse mythology, Sól is the goddess of the sun and Máni is the god of the moon. In this spread, Sól shines her light on what energies are around you, while Máni reflects your emotional world. Choose two runes and place them side by side.

The first rune you draw represents the Gift of Sól. This rune symbolizes your outer self and what is going on in the world around you. Reflect on the meaning of your chosen rune in relation to the outward, seen aspects of your question or situation. For example, this could be in your actions or how you express yourself.

The second rune you choose signifies the Gift of Máni. This rune symbolizes your inner self. Interpret what your selected rune might be telling you about the inward, unseen parts of the situation. This will help you to understand how you truly feel about it.

The Norns' threads spread

The Norns, also called the Nornir, are the most enigmatic and intrinsic beings of the Old Norse mythologies. Very little is written about them, yet their power permeates all life. They are depicted as supernatural weavers of fate and their names are Urðr (meaning "past" or "origin"), Verðandi (meaning "present" or "about"), and Skuld (meaning "future" or "to happen").

The three Norns—Urðr (past), Verðandi (present), and Skuld (future)

In the poem *Völuspá*, from the *Poetic Edda*, the Norns are said to dwell by the well of origin (or of fate/*wyrd*), Urðarbrunnr, at the base of the world tree, Yggdrasil. From this place of power, they shape the ever-unfolding patterns of destiny. It is said in *Snorri's Edda* that the Norns also tend the wounds of Yggdrasil. By mixing water with earth, they make a white clay that heals the bark and branches of the world tree.

In the Viking Age, the bare bones of fate were not something you could necessarily change, and your life and death were set out by the Norns at your birth. However, fulfilling your destiny was one of the most important things you could do, and living up to your soul's potential was one sure way to gain the gods' favor. Although the main aspects of fate were seen as unshakable, there were ways of healing life's tapestry, removing blocks, and influencing the future.

Asking for guidance from the Norns is a powerful experience, and in this three-rune spread, we ask each Norn to share their wisdom. Before beginning this spread, you may wish to meet the Norns with the meditation on pages 108–109. When you are ready, select three runes and lay them in a horizontal line.

1. **Past:** The first rune you choose represents the Thread of Urðr. It brings wisdom and clarity from the past or represents the origin of the situation. This rune may shed light on past events and reveal something that was previously hidden. It could help you to understand what factors led you to your current situation or question.

2. **Present:** The second rune you select signifies the Thread of Verðandi. It brings wisdom and clarity for this present moment, and shares what you might need to know, now. This rune may reveal insights into your current situation or highlight what action is necessary to achieve your desired outcome.

3. **Future:** The third rune you pick symbolizes the Thread of Skuld. It brings wisdom and clarity for the future, and guidance for where your energies may need to be directed. While "future" rune placements are not set in stone, they reveal likely outcomes based on the current trajectory.

PAST   PRESENT   FUTURE

METHODS OF RUNIC DIVINATION **107**

MEDITATION: MEETING THE NORNS

Because the Norns are intertwined with fate, it is helpful for those on a runic path to connect with them. Prepare for this journey to meet the Norns by using the calming and connecting meditations from earlier in the chapter (pages 101–103). You may also wish to record yourself speaking through this meditation, so that you can relax and listen to the recording any time you wish to connect with the Norns.

Don't worry if the Norns aren't that talkative. The Norse gods are quite verbose, but the Norns are a different type of supernatural being—they shape the knowing of the worlds and hold memories of eons, yet they deal with each moment as it happens. They may or may not approach you and speak, but either way, you will receive healing and wisdom simply by being in their presence.

1. Close your eyes and focus on your breath. In your mind's eye, visualize a white mist flowing around your space, swirling around you until all you see is white mist. As the mist begins to clear, you find yourself standing on a plateau looking down over a forested valley. The sound of water surrounds you and you see a waterfall tumbling into the valley below.

2. Looking around, you realize that you are standing upon a vast root of the tree Yggdrasil. You watch the root curve down between the water into the valley before it vanishes into the earth. There is a safe and well-worn path along the root, and you walk down along it. The path follows a stream and leads you into the forest. Notice what season it is as you walk. Are there any animals within the forest? Looking up, you see a raven flying high above the trees. The path curves around and you reach a clearing in the forest.

3. Here, you see a beautifully carved wooden hall, with three doorways. In front of the hall is the well, Urðarbrunnr, its mesmerizing waters silvery white. As you step closer, you become aware of movement from the left door. Urðr emerges from the hall, walking toward you and the well. Perhaps she greets you as she collects water from the well. She gestures for you to follow her as she mixes this sacred water with earth, creating a healing clay. She may speak to you or offer you some of the clay. Spend as long as you wish in the presence of Urðr.

4. You then see movement in the middle door, and witness Verðandi walking into the hall. You say farewell to Urðr, who is consumed in her work, and move toward the second door. Verðandi begins to work at a great weaving loom. Even if she doesn't acknowledge you, she knows you are there, and as the loom weights rhythmically "click" against each other, she begins singing a weaving song. The motion of the threads paired with Verðandi's song is enchanting. Lights and colors dance upon the loom. Perhaps they form the shape of runes, or images.

5. Stay as long as you need and then, when you feel ready to leave Verðandi to her work, silently step out of the door. As you do, you see a figure leave the last door. The woman holds a spear and is walking out toward the trees. This is Skuld, and she stops to see if you are following her. You follow Skuld to the trees, where she begins carving staves of wood. She looks up and smiles and asks if there is something you would like to know. Ask her a question or simply spend time watching her work. She may speak to you as she carves. When she has finished, she hands the carving to you. This stave is carved with runes that will guide you on your onward journey.

6. As you thank her, Skuld looks over into the horizon, and with a flash, she is gone. Holding your stave, you walk back to the well, but there is no one there, except a raven perched on the hall. As you approach, the raven takes flight along the path you came down, and you follow it back. As you walk through the woods by the stream, you begin to see the familiar white mist filling your vision. It swirls around you, until all you can see is the white mist. When it clears once more, you find yourself safely back in your home.

7. Journal your experience and ground yourself by having something to eat or drink.

Urðr

Verðandi

Skuld

METHODS OF RUNIC DIVINATION 109

Elemental rune spread

This four-rune spread works with the four elements to bring balanced guidance to your situation.

- Earth is our home, health, and connection with the physical realm.
- Air is our breath, words, wisdom; what inspires or blocks our minds.
- Fire is our passionate life force, creativity, rage, and spirituality.
- Water is the flow of our emotions; the element of healing and intuition.

Consider your question and ask for guidance from the elements as you select and position four runes, one for each element. (You could use an elemental rune cloth to hold the spread—see page 99.) There are three different ways to interpret this spread, depending on the question.

The first way, (a), is to reflect on what the runes can share with us about our body, mind, spirit, and emotions, allowing us to recognize which aspects of our lives are thriving and which may be blocked. For example, Hagalaz in the Air position could suggest a stressful mental situation, which could lead to transformative thinking, while Isa in the Water position might signal that someone is shutting down their emotions or feeling "frozen."

In the second method, (b), we seek inspiration and guidance on how to best focus our energy. This version of the spread could be done at special occasions, such as seasonal celebrations, or at the beginning of projects.

The final approach, (c), works best for specific, problem-solving readings, because it can offer quick and clear insights into what can be done or understood about a situation.

1. **Earth:**
   (a) Message for the body.
   (b) What needs to grow?
   (c) Practical action.

2. **Air:**
   (a) Message for the mind.
   (b) What feeds my mind?
   (c) Mental focus.

EARTH **AIR**

3. **Fire:**
   (a) Message for the spirit.
   (b) What sparks my spirit?
   (c) Driving force.

4. **Water:**
   (a) Message for emotional self.
   (b) What nourishes my heart?
   (c) Emotional connection.

FIRE **WATER**

The nine branches (or nine worlds) spread

This is a more extended spread for a general reading or to dive into a question. Nine is a significant and recurring number in the mythologies: nine worlds exist within the sacred tree Yggdrasil, Odin hung himself for nine nights, and the god Heimdall is the son of nine mothers. This spread offers wisdom from the realms of Yggdrasil's branches, and guidance from the nine worlds. Select nine runes from the set and position them as in the illustration below. Each placement is aligned with one of the gods or goddesses and holds their counsel and support.

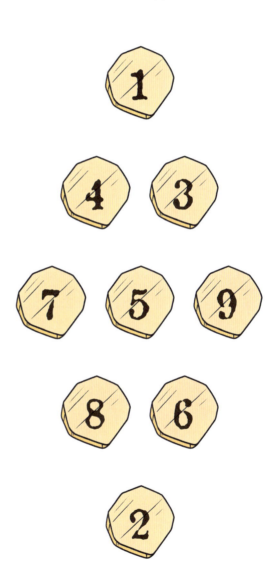

1. **Hopes and aspirations:** Divine siblings Freyja and Freyr guide you on how to manifest your true desires.
2. **Shadows and blocks:** Queen Hel helps you to move through that which holds you back.
3. **Near future:** Baldr, god of light, provides a glimpse of where your current path may be leading you.
4. **Influences from the past:** Wise Mímir reveals how your past might be affecting your present.
5. **Current situation:** Frigg, Queen of Asgard, helps you to understand your present circumstances.
6. **Thoughts and ideas:** Poet Bragi brings guidance about your current mindset.
7. **Wild rune:** Mischievous Loki shows you unexpected influences that may shape your decisions.
8. **Support:** Powerful Thor shows you how or where you can find support.
9. **Road ahead:** All-Father Odin offers guidance for your future direction.

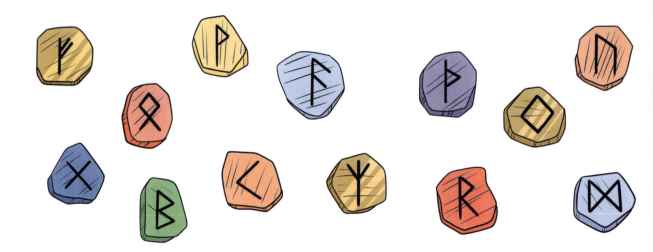

CASTING THE RUNES

Throwing, or casting, the runes is a more complex and intuitive method of divination, and best attempted once you feel confident with the runes and their meanings. For this approach, you will need runes that are simple to throw and a cloth to hold them (page 99). For a shorter or simpler reading, you could choose the number of runes that you wish to include in the reading and take them out of the bag. As you hold the rune bag and choose the runes, focus on the question or situation you would like insight on. For a more in-depth reading, work with the full set of runes.

When reading thrown runes, you will be interpreting both the meaning of the runes and their relationships with each other. When you are ready, hold the runes and cast them on to the cloth.

- Some of the runes will land face up, and these represent the reading's immediate themes.
- The runes that land in the middle of the cloth are central to your question, whereas those on the outskirts may be of lesser importance or signify outlying influences.
- The runes that land face down represent unseen forces, or something that is about to happen.

Because rune throwing is more intuitive than structured spreads, you can choose how you wish to formulate your reading. There is no right or wrong technique for reading runes. Over time and with experimentation, you will find the methods that work best for you.

112 DIVINATION WITH THE RUNES

Reading runes for others

There is no pressure to do readings for others. Many people's journey with the runes is purely a personal one. However, if you do wish to read for others, it can be confidence-building and fulfilling.

One question that people worry about is if they need to be psychic to attempt reading for other people. My answer is no. The runes are filled with enough meaning and wisdom themselves to allow anyone to conduct successful readings. However, it is my belief that everyone is psychic to some degree. We all have a sense of intuition (even if it's a little rusty!) and the more you work with the runes, the more you will hone your own intuitive abilities.

Two traits that I feel are important for a reader are to be compassionate and to have healthy boundaries. Compassion for people's journeys is, hopefully, the main reason we read for others. Although we may get excited to share what we know about the runes, we are essentially there to convey understanding, guidance, and empowerment. That's not to say that we should shy away from the more challenging aspects of a reading. We do need to be honest about what we see, and people will generally appreciate that honesty, especially if it is expressed in a kind and helpful manner.

We must also remember not to take on other people's problems, or to offer our own opinions and advice, however tempting it may be! Unless you have training, a rune reader is not a counselor, and we don't help anyone by taking away the querent's sense of agency. This is where good boundaries come in because they help to protect you and the querent.

Before you set out reading for others, you may wish to consider whether there are any questions or areas you feel uncomfortable looking into. Examples could be health diagnoses, financial decisions, or legal issues, but consider whether there are any other areas that cross your personal boundaries, so that you don't feel under pressure in the moment. Also, considering that the runes are rarely subtle, it might be wise to ask the querent if there are any areas that they are uncomfortable hearing about.

Asking the "right" questions is possibly more important when reading for others, so you may want to talk the querent through ways of formulating their questions. This is a path of exploration and spiritual growth, and although people sometimes think they want dramatic "yes" or "no" answers, in reality the best readings leave the querent feeling empowered to make strong and informed decisions in their own lives.

CHAPTER

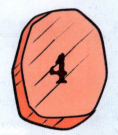

The runic path

Aside from divination, there are many other ways you can work with the runes. This chapter is an invitation to go deeper with your runic path and to adventure with the runes: encounter their energies in nature, harness their powers of healing, and build deeply personal relationships with them.

Creating your own rune set

A simple and fun way of forging a deeper connection with the runes is to make your own rune set. This is achievable for all levels of creative experience.

CHOOSING YOUR MATERIAL

There are various materials you can use to create your rune set and you should consider which one feels right for you. The most commonly used materials are:

- **Wood:** According to the Roman historian Tacitus, wood from fruit- or nut-bearing trees were used for divination. However, you should work with whichever wood resonates with you; all trees are sacred and magic. Check the tree guide (pages 118–119) for inspiration on which tree will suit your magical needs.
- **Clay:** This is a lovely and tactile way of making runes. I like to use white air-drying clay because it reminds me of the white clay that the Norns used to heal the world tree, Yggdrasil (page 107).
- **Pebbles:** Making runes from pebbles is one of the simplest options because they require no special equipment to create or decorate.
- **Sea glass:** Smooth sea glass can be a lovely material for oceanic runes.
- **Crystal:** This is a very beautiful, but more expensive, material for creating runes. If you are feeling adventurous, you could work with the runic crystal correspondences listed in Chapter 2 to create your set.
- **Shells:** I've seen some pretty, iridescent shell runes. Perfect for the sea seer!
- **Card or paper:** Drawing out the runes on pieces of card or paper is a great temporary measure if you are still getting to know the runes and deciding on a more durable material to make your set.

GATHERING YOUR SUPPLIES

You can source the materials for your rune set in different ways. You could buy items from a craft supply store, or gather them while out in nature—you may wish to go for a rune walk, where you go out with the intention of finding your runes, inviting a deity to guide you, if you like. Always check local laws before collecting natural materials and do not take anything from privately owned land without permission.

Remember that nature's gifts come in many forms, and you may not necessarily find the perfect branch (or other material) on your first go. While collecting or creating your rune pieces, try to make sure that they are all a similar size and shape, so that you won't be able to tell them apart when you are using them. It is best to gather a few extra pieces for practicing, or in case any go missing.

The next consideration is which technique you will use to apply the symbols. One option is to use paints or pens. Acrylic paints are especially good, because they can be applied to many different surfaces, are fast-drying, and durable. You could also use acrylic pens or permanent markers. The traditional color for marking the runes is red, however this is not essential, and it can be a lovely, creative process to paint them in the colors that bring *you* joy.

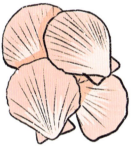

Another method is to carve your runes, if you are working with wood or clay, for example. For wooden runes, you can pick up a pyrography kit reasonably cheaply, and if you are working with clay, you will need some basic clay tools. Take care when using any sharp equipment and get help where needed.

Working with wood

If you decide to use wood, you will need a tree branch that is around 16in (40cm) long and 1–1½in (2.5–4cm) in diameter. Consider whether you would prefer to use a fallen branch or to cut a branch from a tree. If cutting from a tree, ask the tree's permission first and tune in to what the response is. Be prepared to walk away if it doesn't feel right. You could leave a biodegradable offering to the tree spirit after taking the branch. Once you have your branch, use a sharp saw carefully to cut slices with a thickness of approximately ½in (1–1.5cm). Once you have cut your pieces, you may wish to use sandpaper to smooth the surfaces.

Take care when working with wood. It isn't advisable to work with yew, especially if you are inexperienced with woodwork, because the wood is poisonous. Other trees, such as holly, have poisonous berries. Be careful when using saws or other sharp equipment; it would be wise to ask someone who works with wood to help you.

CREATING YOUR OWN RUNE SET

MAGICAL TREE GUIDE

Although I am a huge advocate for following your intuition, it can be helpful to learn a little bit about the trees you are working with if you are creating wooden runes. Here is a quick guide to tree lore, including the Norse deities and types of magic associated with each tree. It is by no means exhaustive or rigid, so please feel free to add your own correspondences and favorite trees to the list!

Alder
Deities: Mímir, Ægir, Rán, Njörðr
Magic: Divination, Protection, Healing, Trusting Intuition, Spiritual Warrior

Apple
Deities: Iðunn, Freyja
Magic: Immortality, Eternal Youth, Love, Faerie Connection, Fertility, Prosperity

Ash
Deities: Odin, Frigg, Norns, Hel
Magic: The World Tree (Yggdrasil), Intellect, Inner and Outer Realities, Initiation

Birch
Deities: Freyja, Frigg, Urðr, Loki
Magic: New Beginnings, Growth, Purification, Healing, Otherworld Connection, Inspiration

Cherry
Deities: Týr, Skaði, Freyja
Magic: Action, Success, Love, Divination, Spiritual Awakening, Faerie Connection

Elder
Deities: The Mother Goddess, Hel
Magic: Healing, Rebirth, Magical Knowledge, Earth Wisdom

Elm
Deities: Freyja, Frigg, Gullveig, Odin, Loki, Hel
Magic: Love, Connection with Elves and the Underworld, Purification, Wisdom

Hazel
Deity: Freyja
Magic: Love, Attraction, Playful Wisdom, Divination, Dowsing, Fertility, Inspiration

118 THE RUNIC PATH

Holly
Deities: Týr, Freyr, Ullr
Magic: Protection, Luck, Intellect, Courage, Dream Magic

Linden
Deities: Freyja, Odin, Týr
Magic: Love, Protection, Prosperity, Luck, Immortality

Maple
Deity: Freyr
Magic: Communication, Celebrations, Prosperity, Creativity

Oak
Deity: Thor
Magic: Strength, Doorway to the Otherworld, Ancestry, Loyalty, Courage, Wisdom

Pine
Deities: Hermóðr, Njörðr, Odin
Magic: Purification, Fertility, Protection, Prosperity, Resilience

Rowan
Deities: Thor, Frigg, Freyja
Magic: Protection Against Magic, Healing, Purity, Psychic Powers

Walnut
Deity: Thor
Magic: Strength, Protection, Inner and Outer Riches, Spiritual Awakening

Willow
Deity: Máni
Magic: Healing, Lunar Magic, Divination, Soothing Emotions, Water Magic

Yew
Deity: Ullr, Skaði, Odin, Hel
Magic: Transformation, Ancestral Magic

CREATING YOUR OWN RUNE SET

MAKING YOUR RUNES

Once you have gathered all your materials, it's time to create your sacred space for the rune-making process. You can do this by visualizing or casting a circle of light around your space, or you could sing the runes and visualize them creating a circle around you. Invite a deity to join your creative process, if you like; you could even dedicate your runes to them—now or at a later date.

Before marking your rune pieces, it's a good idea to write the runic alphabet out a couple of times to get used to the feel of the shapes. When you are ready, intone the runes and then mark the symbols on to your rune pieces, one by one. Don't worry about your runes looking perfect; they *will* be perfect, faults and all. The most important thing is the love and energy you put in to creating them.

When you have marked your runes, you will want to charge them up with energy. You could place your hand over them and chant the runes; visualize light going in to them; place them under the full moon or rising sun; or, my favorite technique, drum energy into them. You may also want to seal your runes—beeswax works well on wooden runes and paint varnish is good for pebbles. Give thanks to any deities you invoked and ask them to bless your runes.

Close your space by visualizing your circle closing and any light going back in to the earth. Sing or chant the runes once more but imagine them departing your space as you do so. Finally, you will now want a home for your runes, which could be a small bag or box (page 98). You could either buy or make your chosen container, and then cleanse or bless it before placing your runes inside.

If you like, you could create your runes over a longer period of time. Making and working with one rune per day for twenty-four days will help you to gain lived experience of each runic energy. Alternatively, a longer-term project is to create one rune per month and dedicate each month to working with that rune's energy.

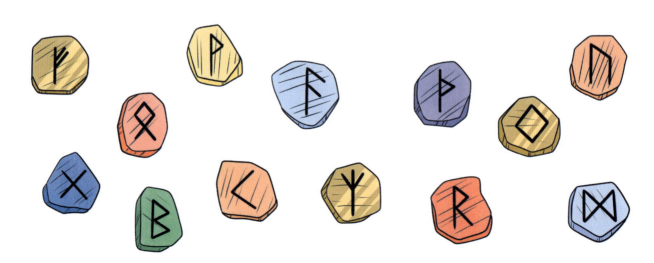

There are places in between
Sometimes hidden in a dream
Shimmering lands of mist and rhyme
A space between your heart and mine

Meeting the runes in nature

Connecting with the runes in nature's wild places acts as a bridge between our inner and outer worlds. It is also fun, empowering, and completely free!

Over the next few pages, I will share a few suggestions for different kinds of runic walks, rituals, and connections that you can try while out in nature, which will hopefully support your practice and root your wisdom in to the land.

WITCH WALKS

The simplest way to connect with the runic energies in nature is to go out for a "witch walk," and ask for guidance from the land. A witch walk is what I call an intuitive walk, wander, or experience that opens us up to the spirits of the land (page 126) and invites the gods and guides to bring insights and wild wisdom. Witch walks can be as ritualistic or as simple as you choose. This is something you can do on a lunch break, or it is a practice you can really take your time over and relax into over a full day.

You will want to travel light but take enough to ensure your comfort. You may have a sacred item that you wish to hold or wear while walking, such as a staff, a piece of jewelry, or a healing pouch. This isn't essential but it might help focus your energy and intentions. The only rule I hold about these walks is that they allow for an opportunity to switch off from our internal dialogue and to learn true presence with our surroundings.

Witch walks are opportunities to set an intention and open us up to a deeper relationship with the earth and all her beings, allowing the land to speak to us through symbols, signs, weather, and animal and plant life. Before you set out, consider what your intention is. Would you like guidance on a particular issue? Are you looking to connect with the spirit or energies of a specific place? Are you looking to get to know the runes a little better? Or are you wishing to connect with the gods through the land? If you are unable to get out for a walk, you can still receive messages and develop awareness while seated in the garden or by observing what you see and feel from a window. The practice on pages 124–125 gives you some ideas for what you could look out for.

If there is a rune that you are learning about or working with, you could invite it on your walk by intoning it, drawing it on to your body, or carrying an image of it with you. Allow the rune to guide your walk and reveal something to you. The same applies for if you are getting to know a deity, tree spirit, ancestor, or animal guide. Trust yourself and remember that messages can come through all aspects of nature.

All witch walks are deeply personal and, as long as you follow your intuition and respect the land and your own safety, then you are witch walking perfectly right! At the end of any witch walk, remember to give thanks to the spirits of the land, the gods, and guides for all of your blessings.

PRACTICE: READING RUNES IN THE LAND

This practice is an invitation for the runes to offer you guidance on a question or area of interest or concern, allowing them to speak to you specifically through the land.

1. Focus on your question, holding it clearly in your mind, and ask to be shown the runes and signs that will support you. The clearer the question, the easier it will be to see the guidance. Decide whether you wish this guidance to come through while on a walk or during the course of your day, and be open to how these answers will turn up. When you are ready, set out on your walk or embark on your daily activities.

2. Look out for the signs and messages that the land may be trying to share with you. For me, the most common way I find runes in the land is through fallen twigs or branches that create runic shapes, but there is no limit to how nature can show us these messages. You may receive messages in:

   - The types of trees you encounter
   - The shapes of plants, leaves, and seaweed
   - The birds you encounter—notice their song, or flight patterns
   - Other animals you meet and their behavior
   - Patterns in the soil left by animals
   - Markings and patterns in rocks and pebbles
   - Markings in the sand when the tide has gone out
   - Creatures in rock pools
   - Shapes seen in waterfalls
   - Swirling water in rivers
   - Cloud shapes
   - Constellations in the night sky
   - Any repetitive image or message that comes through, no matter how "unspiritual" it may initially seem!

124 THE RUNIC PATH

Signs from the leaves and trees   Messages from animals   Guidance from the stars

The weather you experience and the "mood" of the place you visit might also share information relevant to your question. You do not have to be in a beautiful place to receive messages. I have had some very clear guidance come through while stuck in traffic by observing the signs and pictures on vans driving past or from billboard advertisements!

3. As soon as you safely can, note down the messages and signs you receive, and don't worry if they do not initially make sense. Some signs will leap out at you while others will take longer to process and comprehend. You are creating and developing your own language with the land and the runes, so trust your instincts and be patient with yourself. By keeping a journal of your questions, messages, and how the situation turned out, you will grow in confidence with your readings and understanding of the runes.

MEETING THE RUNES IN NATURE   125

LAND SPIRITS

Working with runes in the landscape helps us to connect with the spirits of the land, known as *landvættir* in Old Norse paganism. Unfortunately, we have mostly forgotten how to acknowledge or commune with land spirits. In older pagan times, these spirits, which include animal and tree spirits, ancestors, elves, and even the gods themselves, were used to receiving gifts and friendship from humans. Even if people didn't want to work with the land spirits, they certainly knew that they existed and did their best not to offend them! These otherworldly beings often dwell within the land—in hollow hills, in rivers, and in stone. We sometimes sense their presence in the "between" times and places—on misty mornings, or in the woods at twilight.

If you encounter the land spirits while on a witch walk, greet them and show your care for the place by leaving a biodegradable and nontoxic offering, or by making a promise to perhaps clear litter in the area or get involved with an environmental project. On a smaller scale, a gift can be a poem or a song, either of which is usually gratefully received. Promises made to land spirits and faeries are sacred—never make them lightly. Please do not offer anything that you might forget you promised or aren't prepared to do. For obvious reasons, the spirits of the land are often wary of humans and so with this magical work we are building a bridge of trust and companionship between the worlds. If you take care of the land and leave a space as you found it, or even tidier than you found it, the land spirits will gladly welcome you back.

RUNES IN THE URBAN LANDSCAPE

Witch walks can be held in urban areas as well as in wilder places. This may feel a little more challenging at first, because surely it must be harder to sense the energies of the runes while contending with rush hour traffic? The answer is both yes and no! Although the runes express natural and primal elements, they can also represent a multitude of human experiences.

Towns and cities are usually ancient places teeming with history just beneath the sidewalk. I lived in London for ten years and felt so much magic walking through the parks, along the rivers, and through the streets of the old city. As we wander along these well-trodden paths, we awaken a place's memory and magic, which in turn awakens something within us.

EXPERIENCE: MAGIC ON THE MOORS

Here is one of my own witch-walk experiences, which I hope will inspire your journeys. As I got out of my car at one of my favorite soul places, I immediately heard the low gurgling croak of ravens above. Although this is not unusual, I paid extra attention, because I knew that this was the first sign of my walk. Sure enough, one of the ravens swooped down, perched upon a fence pole, and started making complex sounds that I hadn't heard before. As I slowly moved closer, the raven continued calling out and was completely unphased by my presence.

After watching for a while, I began my onward journey and had planned to head toward an outcrop where I saw some wild ponies in the distance. The ravens, however, had other plans as they flew overhead in the opposite direction toward the Bronze Age round barrows. Feeling a pull in my chest to walk the ravens' path, I turned and followed them past the barrow mounds and up the hill to its summit. It was like they were playing hide and seek with me—they would vanish out of view and then reappear beside me, leaping from the heather and soaring up the path.

I followed until I reached a second burial mound, and there they flew off playfully into the distance and I felt the pull within me shift. Leaving the ravens, I descended the hill toward the ponies. Approaching them, I spotted the heavily pregnant mare that I had been concerned about the previous week. She seemed to remember me and approached me happily, resting her muzzle in my hand. Her eyes were calm, wise, and kind. We both stood there for a while, feeling a warm gentleness in the wintery wild, until she was ready to move on and rejoin her herd.

There was so much to contemplate and be grateful for in this journey. The magic of the ravens was undoubtedly connected with Odin via the playful flight of his ravens Huginn and Muninn. The runes I associated with this part of the walk were Ansuz and Mannaz for the divine communication, and Othala in connection with the ancestral tombs. These runes are all associated with the All-Father, Odin. Descending from the hilltop mound to the pregnant mare, I considered Berkano as the feminine rune of the tomb and the birthing womb, and Ehwaz for my bond with the mare. Although this part of the witch walk felt deeply feminine, I can't escape the symbolism of Loki in mare form, pregnant with Odin's future steed, Sleipnir.

MEETING THE RUNES IN NATURE 127

If we sing the runes to the land,
the land sings back to us its own ancient song...

Singing the runes

By singing or chanting the runes, you will become more familiar with their names and feel their energies reverberating in your body. Singing the runes also honors them and the gods, and calls their power to you.

A powerful daily practice is to sing through the whole Elder Futhark, three times if possible. (Refer to the suggested pronunciations in Chapter 2.) Take your time singing each rune, visualizing it in your mind, and attuning with its unique energy. Experiment by voicing it in different ways. Does it feel right to sing it softly? Or is it a rune that requires you to make some noise? Remember that this is your own personal journey of exploration and there are no wrong answers. If you live in a busy house, you could sing the runes in the car, shower, or anywhere you can find privacy!

Notice whether you sense any colors or experience any physical or emotional sensations as you sing. If you are working with a particular rune, look up its correspondences in Chapter 2 and perhaps wear the associated colors, visualize the associated animals, or hold a relevant crystal in your hand as you sing. You could even sing the rune into the crystal, so that it becomes a conductor for that rune's healing power.

GALDR

Galdr is a magical Old Scandinavian technique using the voice, which includes chants, songs, and incantations. It is a way of using our voices to create a sacred space and call the spirits, ancestors, or guides to us. In the *Saga of Erik the Red*, a traveling seeress, or *völva*, known as Thorbjörg Litilvölva was invited to perform a *seiðr* rite at a settlement. *Seiðr* is a type of ecstatic trance prophecy in which the seeress seeks answers from the spirits and ancestors. For the ritual to occur, Thorbjörg declared that the women were required to sing the ritual songs, but none was initially able or willing. The song was essential for calling in the spirits and allowing Thorbjörg to reach a trance state. Fortunately, a woman named Gudrid relented. Her singing was so beautiful that, according to Thorbjörg, many spirits were present and were charmed by her voice.

This story reminds us of the powerful and partly forgotten art of song and the healing power of the voice. In modern culture, we hold a false belief that if we don't sound like a professional singer, then we should simply keep quiet. However, our voices are healing tools that offer us the ability to express ourselves, to release blocks, and to call that which we need toward us. Our voices are powerhouses of transformation, and the runes invite us to experiment, play, and heal through the power of our own personal song.

SINGING THE RUNES TO THE LAND

We can use *galdr* to help us feel the energy of the runes within our bodies, but we can also use it to connect with and honor the land. Hopefully you already have places in your local landscape that feel sacred to you. If not, regular witch walking (pages 121–127) will help you to discover those places that bring healing and sing to your soul. These special places could be stone circles, woodlands, streams, beaches, cairns, or anywhere else that nurtures your spirit.

When you find your personal power places, you can build greater connections with the land spirits (page 126) by visiting them regularly and by singing the runes to them. For example, you might wish to sing Berkano to a birch wood, Eihwaz to an ancient yew tree, Laguz to bodies of water, or Fehu to a growing sapling. If there is a place where you wish to hold rituals, you may want to explore intoning or chanting all of the runes while visualizing their energies in order to create a sacred circle.

Visit your personal power places at potent times, such as on new and full moons, and on the wheel of the year's festival days (the eight annual pagan celebrations). Observe how the land and the energy shift at different times. What does this teach you about the runes you are connecting with? What does the land whisper to you as you connect with it on a deeper level? You could create a natural seasonal altar or mandala to invoke the runes, using any natural materials you have found, such as leaves, twigs, flowers, and shells. After creating your space and working with your *galdr*, sit or stand in mediation and let the land and its spirits commune with you.

Remember, *galdr* in this sense is a conversation between you and spirit. It isn't a performance unless you would like it to be. Singing in nature does increase the chances of people hearing you, and there have been several times where I've been belting out a song and some bemused walkers have ambled past! Gently humming and intoning the runes works just as well as a rock-opera-style rendition. It is the intention, focus, and energy that counts more than the volume. Singing to the land reconnects us with our wild and vital essence, and it also helps us to reawaken our sacred bond with the earth.

Healing with the runes

Runes are powerhouses of wisdom, and gateways that enable us to access primal and cosmic forces of creation, growth, connection, and transformation. Working with the runes for healing can support our physical, mental, emotional, and spiritual well-being.

RUNE HEALING IN THE SAGAS AND POEMS

Nowadays, the runes are mainly known for their powers of divination (see Chapter 3), but this was not always the case. The Icelandic sagas and Eddic poetry share that runes were once mostly used for healing charms, protection, blessings, and spell work. In the poem *Hávamál*, from the *Poetic Edda*, Odin lists eighteen rune spells, ranging from spells to aid physical healing and protect warriors to necromancy and seducing lovers.

In *Sigrdrífumál*, part of the *Poetic Edda*, the wise Valkyrie Sigrdrífa tutored the hero Sigurd on rune charms and healing. She offered him a drink of beer filled with spells and runes of pleasure, and continued to describe to him an array of different rune charms. Some examples of these rune charms included preventing poisoning, helping mothers to give birth, sailing safely across the seas, ensuring victory and loyalty, and gaining wisdom.

The two Merseburg Charms are the only Old High German pagan poems that have been recorded. The second charm concerns how the gods and goddesses used spells to heal Baldr's lame horse. The goddesses Frija (Frigg), Fulla, Sunna, and Sinthgunt, followed by the god Wodan (Odin), all charmed the horse, fixing its bones and healing the wound with the use of their incantations.

A further example of runic healing appears in *Egil's Saga*. This Icelandic saga depicts Egil as a powerful rune master who is asked to heal a sick girl. He discovers that the previous healer carved the wrong runes on to the girl's bed, thus making her illness worse. Egil removed and remedied the runes, and the girl immediately began to recover.

These stories remind us that, as we connect with the runes on a deeper level, we can allow their energies to work with us and empower our own healing journeys.

HOW TO APPROACH RUNIC HEALING

We can work with the runes to encourage energy flow and well-being in our bodies, as well as to work through mental and emotional blocks. Obviously, none of this guidance replaces going to a doctor or relevant medical professional, but hopefully it will assist and inspire your path of healing and wholeness.

Each of the runes provide different aspects of magic and healing, and we can access their energies by applying their runic symbols to our bodies—by anointing with oils or drawing with body paints or pens—and also to our belongings. Here are some ideas to experiment with:

- Receive communication from the gods, Odin in particular, by drawing or anointing Ansuz (pages 34–35) on to your third eye (located between your eyebrows), your throat, or your hands.
- For safe journeys, anoint or draw Raidho (pages 36–38) on to yourself, your vehicle, or a travel ticket.
- Anoint your forehead or hands with Algiz (pages 64–66) for divine protection.
- For justice in legal situations, draw or trace Teiwaz (pages 72–73) on to your legal documents.
- Anoint or draw Ehwaz (pages 77–79) on to your hands for a positive connection with animals, especially horses.
- Connect with the ancestors by anointing or drawing Othala (pages 88–90) on to your feet as you walk the earth, or on to your hands as you connect with memories of the past.

You could also work with two runes at a time to amplify their healing energy. For example, Fehu and Uruz add healing strength to other runes. Certain runes are "general healing runes," and we will explore their healing properties in more detail over the next few pages.

132   THE RUNIC PATH

Fehu for sensuality and self-love

As a rune of life-force energy and vitality, Fehu (pages 26–27) is a wonderful, all-purpose healing rune. It helps us to connect with our body and our own sensual power. As a rune of abundance, Fehu doesn't distinguish between the flow of money and the flow of self-love. If you are feeling a lack in your finances, you could also be struggling with underlying issues involving self-care and self-worth.

Healing practice

You can work with Fehu to increase energy levels, release anxiety, and bring awareness back into your body.

1. Stand up, if possible, and feel the connection of your feet upon the earth.
2. Chant or sing Fehu, and visualize golden energy coming up from the core of the earth, rising through the land, and up in to your feet. Feel this golden light flowing up through your body and nourishing every part of you.
3. Now, visualize golden rays of the sun shining down on you, warming your body. As this energy flows, you may feel your arms raise up.
4. This golden light nourishes your heart, and you feel a beautiful green or pink light shining in your chest. Feel the warmth of Fehu lighting up and energizing your body and soul.
5. Stay in this space for as long as you wish, then allow any extra energy to be released back in to the earth.
6. Place your hands on your heart and breathe deeply, thanking Freyja and Fehu.

Affirmation

I am love. I am vibrant. I am life. I am worthy. I am golden.

Anointments

- With your favorite warm, sensual, or spicy oil, draw the Fehu rune on to the skin over your heart to encourage self-love and passion.
- I like to anoint my forehead with the double Fehu rune, which also creates a double Algiz. This helps to connect me with Freyja and the Valkyries, and to my higher self.
- You could anoint your mirror with Fehu, look at your wonderful reflection, and speak the above affirmation. Do this for a period of nine days, or a multiple of nine, because the number nine is sacred to Freyja.
- To encourage a positive flow of wealth, anoint your wallet with Fehu.

Uruz for strength

Uruz (pages 28–30) is the archetypal healing rune, and it supports strength, healing, cleansing, and endurance. It is a rune to call upon when you need to fight off an illness and boost your immune system. Singing Uruz can strengthen your resolve and support your body's healing process. Because Uruz is a cleansing rune, it is good to chant it in the shower while visualizing all you wish to release being washed away.

Healing practice

For this healing practice, you will be making the shape of Uruz with your body. There are a couple of ways you can do this, so don't worry if they aren't both accessible to you.

Option 1

1. Stand flat upon the earth and draw energy up into your feet like you did in the Fehu healing practice (page 133).
2. When you are ready, intone the Uruz rune and then bend over forward with a flat back, and reach your hands down to the floor. Don't worry if they don't touch the earth.
3. Breathe deeply and visualize the orange, brown, or deep red colors of Uruz flowing through your body.

Although it isn't strictly Uruz-shaped, I prefer to do this position as a "downward dog" yoga posture.

Option 2

1. Stand, sit, or lie on the floor and make the Uruz "horns" with your hands by imagining you are at a rock concert! Hold your index and little fingers pointed out to make the horns and then use your thumb to hold down your middle and ring fingers.
2. Hold your Uruz "finger horns" above your head or touch them to the earth and feel the powerful and determined energy of Uruz flowing through you.
3. Intone Uruz in a deep and strong voice.

Affirmation

I am strong. I am healing. I am healthy. I endure.

Anointment

Bless your food with the Uruz rune. You won't need any oils for this, unless you want to use olive oil! Just using your finger, your voice, and your intention, you can power up your meals by anointing Uruz over the dish. Visualize the rune's strength and healing going into the food, and then into your body as you eat it.

Sowilo for warmth

The healing sun of Sowilo (pages 67–69) brings warmth, creativity, and optimism into our lives. When the weight of the world feels too heavy, or grief has made us lose our way, working with the Sowilo rune can remind us of our inner light and help us move forward once more.

Sowilo's healing feels like the sun breaking through dark clouds. It is the relief of the land or sea transformed by the sun's rays and warmth returning to our world. The light of Sowilo reminds us that hope is always available to us and even the darkest nights will pass. Working with this rune for healing encourages us to trust ourselves, our path, and our connections to the divine.

Healing practices

There are several ways you can work with Sowilo to help you feel brighter and to bring a sense of positivity and hope in to your life.

- Use solar colors, such as yellow, orange, or red, to draw or paint Sowilo on to paper or canvas as a symbol of the light, hope, and positive energy in your life.
- Wear gold, bronze, brass, or copper to connect with the sun's power.
- Gently move your body to help release grief and move any trapped emotions. Sowilo's shape is reminiscent of a moving snake and encourages us to gently sway our bodies. Snakes hold the symbolism of healing and rebirth, which can be helpful when working with the Sowilo rune. Try moving your hips in a circle or a figure-eight shape. Perhaps undulate your arms as if they were snakes.
- Place your hands on your stomach and sing the Sowilo rune. If you are lacking faith in your path, this practice will help you to connect with your intuition.

Affirmation

I am light. I trust my path. I thrive.

Anointment

To support healing with Sowilo, intone the rune and anoint it on to your body where you feel you need hope and warmth the most. You could anoint all your chakras (see page 140) to bring light and energy to your whole being.

Berkano for new beginnings

Berkano (pages 74–76) has healing power associated with all aspects of birthing, nurturing, and stepping into new phases of life. It is obviously a rune that you, your family, or birthing partner can sing and chant if you are in the physical process of labor—especially the first syllable, "ber." Berkano's mothering energies remind us of mother bears, and intoning this rune can invoke the powerful protective spirit of the bear.

Healing practice

You can work with Berkano for healing, blessing, and connecting with the womb, or with your creative spark.

1. Sit with your legs crossed and gently sing Berkano while slowly moving your torso in a circle. You could either place your hands over your pelvic area or rest them on your knees.
2. Imagine you are stirring a cauldron—your spine being the spoon and your pelvis being the cauldron. Each time you rotate and chant Berkano, visualize pouring some good magic in to the cauldron as you stir! You could stir all your wishes in to the cauldron, or you could focus on the things you are grateful for.
3. When you are ready to stop, return to center and sit in stillness with your hands over your lower tummy.
4. Chant Berkano three more times. Breathe deeply and release.

Affirmation

I am held. I am life. I create. I am nourished.

Anointments

- Because it is a rune of fertility, you could anoint or use body paint to draw Berkano on to your body to enhance fertility.
- For inspiring new projects and ideas, chant Berkano and anoint your third eye (located between your eyebrows).
- Draw Berkano on to your notebooks or sketchbooks to bless new projects. Birch trees have a papery bark that often peels—if you find some, paint the rune on to it or write your new project or idea on to the birch paper and place it on your altar or in your working area.

Laguz for emotions

As a rune of water, Laguz (pages 82–84) is one of the fundamental healing runes and supports all endeavors of cleansing and diving deep into our emotions. Although I don't focus on reversed readings in this book, when I receive an upside-down Laguz, I know that, like a fishing hook, Laguz will be plunging the depths to find some unhealed wound, or emotional block, and bringing it up to the surface to be healed. It is an uncomfortable process, but, ultimately, completely worth it.

Healing practice

You can work with Laguz to help you connect with your emotions and your intuition.

1. Sitting cross-legged, or upright on a chair, place your hands on your stomach and take some deep breaths. Visualize your spine as the long vertical line of Laguz and your head as the shorter line at the top.
2. Inhale and feel your breath draw up through your head, then exhale down through your spine and into your stomach. You may wish to whisper "la" as you inhale and "guz" as you exhale.
3. Repeat this for at least a minute and then sit in stillness for a while, allowing your thoughts to flow in and out of your consciousness.

Affirmation

I am flow. I am fate. I am blessed. I release.

Anointments

- For emotional flow and cleansing, draw or anoint the rune on to your body and sing Laguz. While doing so, imagine the light and colors of Laguz flowing through and around you like water. If you can do this while near or in a body of water, such as a waterfall, stream, or even the shower, all the better!
- With your finger, draw Laguz over your drink to bless the liquid you are drinking.

HEALING WITH THE RUNES

MEDITATION: INVOKING THE RUNES

Within this book, we have learned many ways to work with the runes. Whether you are seeking knowledge, healing, or a connection with their ancient power, this simple meditation exercise offers a way to invoke the energy of a particular rune into your sacred space for meditation and exploration.

1. Make sure you are somewhere you won't be disturbed, then set up your space; light a candle or incense, if you like. You can sit or stand.

2. When you are comfortable, take some deep, calming breaths and envision yourself drawing energy up from the earth in to your body. With each in-breath, focus on the life-giving energy you are inhaling, and with each out-breath, exhale all that is ready to leave. Relax into this space for as long as you wish.

3. When your body feels full of energy, use your dominant hand to reach out in front of you and draw your chosen rune in the air, while powerfully intoning or chanting the rune three times.

4. As you visualize the rune in front of you, look at its light and its colors. These colors could be the same as the correspondences given in Chapter 2, but don't worry if not, because this is your own personal connection with the rune.

5. Breathe in the energy of the rune and notice what it looks, sounds, and feels like. Is the rune moving or growing in front of you? Perhaps the rune has leaves or rays of light growing from it, or you see or hear an animal. Allow this experience to be as complex or as simple as it needs to be. Imagine yourself stepping closer to bask in the rune's energy.

6. When you are ready, visualize the rune's energy diminishing and fading away. You could also use your hands to "close" the rune's gateway. Sit or stand in stillness for a while, then thank the runes and journal your experience.

Conclusion

May the wisdom of the runes inspire your beautiful mind.
May the healing of the runes support you:
body, heart, and soul.
May you remember the stories of the gods, the songs
of the ancestors, and the power of the sacred land.

Reading the runes is an ever-spiraling path of wisdom, healing, and remembering. Sing the runes, cast them, and read, write, and create with them. Root your wisdom deep into the earth and allow the runes to open gateways of myth, adventure, and understanding in your life. As you close this book, know that new chapters are beginning, and all the worlds are awaiting your magic.

Odin stands between the roots of Yggdrasil, just beyond the shores of night. His one seeing eye gleams with the light of a thousand stars. He throws a stone into the air, and you catch it. A rune dances upon its surface. The All-Father gives you a knowing smile and turns away, vanishing among the leaves of Yggdrasil.

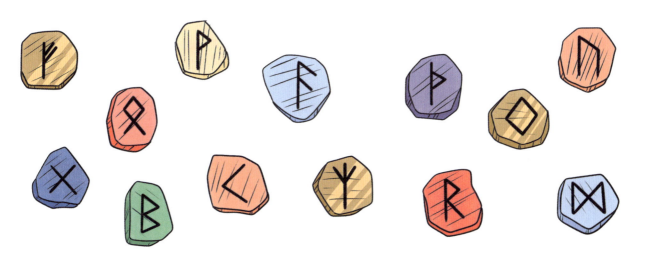

Glossary

Æsir: The tribe of gods (led by Odin) that is mentioned most frequently in the Old Norse source texts.

Ætt: The name given to each of the three sets of eight runes in the Elder Futhark alphabet.

All-Father: One of the many titles given to the god Odin.

Anointment: The application of oil to the skin (or an item) for healing purposes.

Chakras: The seven major energy points in the body.

Gylfaginning: Meaning "The Deluding of Gylfi," the first main prose of *Snorri's Edda*.

Hamr: Meaning one's "shape" or "skin," an aspect, often a feathered cloak, that can aid shape-shifting. The goddess Freyja's *válshamr* transforms the wearer into a falcon or hawk.

Hávamál: Meaning "Sayings of the High One," a poem containing social wisdom, spells, and runic charms, usually attributed to Odin.

Jötnar (sing. jötunn): Primal and powerful beings who ruled before the gods and are often hostile toward them. Synonymous with "giants."

Kennings: Metaphors used in Old Norse poetry to describe words and names. For example, instead of saying "the sea," one could say "the whale road."

Poetic Edda: The collection of Old Norse/Icelandic mythological and historical poetry, recounting tales from the beginning of time to the events of Ragnarök.

Querent: Someone who asks questions and seeks answers from divination methods.

Ragnarök: A cataclysmic battle that led to the ultimate destruction of the world.

Saga: Any type of medieval Icelandic prose.

Seiðr: A type of magical trance prophecy specific to Scandinavia.

Sigrdrífumál: Meaning "The Lay of Sigrdrífa," an Eddic poem about the Valkyrie Sigrdrífa.

Skáldskaparmál: The second part of *Snorri's Edda*, consisting of a dialogue between the sea god, Ægir, and Bragi, god of poetry.

Snorri's Edda (Prose Edda): The most detailed source of pre-Christian Scandinavian cosmology and mythology, compiled by Icelandic poet and historian, Snorri Sturluson.

Urðarbrunnr: One of the three wells that sits beneath Yggdrasil. Also known as the well of fate, *wyrd*, memory, or origin, it is associated with the three Norns (weavers of fate), especially Urðr, meaning "past" or "origin."

Valkyries: Meaning "choosers of the slain," beings who can shape-shift into bird form and carry those who die in battle to the afterlife.

Vanir: The second tribe of Germanic gods mentioned in the mythologies, associated with the land, agriculture, and fertility.

Völundarkviða: Meaning "The Poem of Volund," the tragic tale of Wayland the Smith and his swan maiden lover, recorded in the *Poetic Edda*.

Völuspá: Meaning "The Prophecy of the Seeress," the first poem of the *Poetic Edda*, describing the creation of the world and events up to and beyond Ragnarök.

Wild Hunt: A phantom horde of nocturnal riders who journey across the winter skies, led by a god or goddess.

Wyrd: An Anglo-Saxon concept related to fate and destiny, linked to the modern English word, "weird."

Yggdrasil: The mighty, sacred tree that sits at the center of the nine worlds and connects all life. Also known as the world tree or the tree of life.

Bibliography and resources

Primary sources

Byock, J. (ed. and trans.) (2005) *Snorri Sturluson, The Prose Edda*. London: Penguin.

Crawford, J. (ed. and trans.) (2019) *The Wanderer's Hávamál*. Indianapolis: Hackett Publishing Company Inc.

Finlay, A. and Faulkes, A. (ed. and trans.) (2011) *Snorri Sturluson Heimskringla Volume I*. London: Viking Society for Northern Research, University College London.

Kunz, K. (trans.) *Eirik the Red's Saga* in Thorsson, Ö. (ed.) (2000) *The Sagas of the Icelanders*. London: Penguin.

Larrington, C. (ed. and trans.) (2014) *The Poetic Edda*. 2nd edn. Oxford: Oxford University Press.

Pettit, E. (ed. and trans.) (2023) *The Poetic Edda: A Dual-Language Edition*. Cambridge: Open Book Publishers.

Secondary sources

Bek-Pedersen, K. (2011) *The Norns in Old Norse Mythology*. Edinburgh: Dunedin Academic Press.

Brink, S. and Price, N. (ed.) (2008) *The Viking World*. Oxon: Routledge.

Jennbert, K. (2011) *Animals and Humans: Recurrent Symbiosis in Archaeology and Old Norse Religion*. Sweden: Nordic Academic Press.

Kvilhaug, M. (2020) *The Seed of Yggdrasill*. USA/Canada: The Three Little Sisters.

Price, N. (2019) *The Viking Way: Magic and Mind in Late Iron Age Scandinavia*. Oxford: Oxbow Books.

Price, N. (2020) *The Children of Ash and Elm: A History of the Vikings*. London: Allen Lane.

Simek, R. (2007) *Dictionary of Northern Mythology*. 5th edn. Cambridge: D.S. Brewer.

Online resources

The Anglo-Saxon Rune Poem. Available at The English Companions website: www.tha-engliscan-gesithas.org.uk

The Rune Poems. Available at Ragnar's Ragweed Forge website: www.ragweedforge.com/poems.html

Runor (Swedish National Heritage Board's runic inscriptions database): https://app.raa.se/open/runor/search

Modern rune studies

Cunningham, M. R. *Magin Rose*. Available at: www.maginrose.com

Fries, J. (2006) *Helrunar: A Manual of Rune Magick*. 3rd edn. Oxford: Mandrake.

Gerrard, K. (2009) *Odin's Gateways: A Practical Guide to the Wisdom of the Runes Through Galdr, Sigils and Casting*. London: Avalonia.

Kincaid, I. (2019) *Lost Teachings of the Runes: Northern Mysteries and the Wheel of Life*. USA: Red Wheel/Weiser.

Paxson, D. L. (2005) *Taking Up the Runes: A Complete Guide to Using Runes in Spells, Divination, and Magic*. USA: Red Wheel/Weiser.

Pollington, S. (2022) *Rudiments of Runelore*. 3rd edn. UK: Anglo-Saxon Books.

Thorsson, E. (2020) *Futhark: A Handbook of Rune Magic*. USA: Red Wheel/Weiser.

Index

Page references for glossary entries are italicized.

abundance 26–7, 56–8, 85–7, 133
achievement 45, 67–9, 92
Æsir gods 14, 24, 70, 80, *140*
Ætts 11, 22–3, *140*
 Freyja and Freyr's Ætt 23, 24–45
 Heimdall's Ætt 46–69
 Týr's Ætt 70–93
aggression 31–3
Alfheim 14, 86
Algiz (Z) 64–6
All-Father *140 see also* Odin
alphabets 10–12, 22–3
altars 35, 130
ancestors 88–90, 126, 128, 132
Ansuz (A) 34–5
Asgard 14, 32, 46
Auðumbla 13, 26
aurochs 28–30
awakening 76, 91–2

beginnings 74–6, 91–2, 136
belonging 44–5, 88–90
Berkano (B) 74–6, 136
birch trees 74–6, 136
birth 61–3, 74–6, 136
blank rune 93
Bragi 39–41
breath work 35, 43
Buri 13, 26, 28

celebration 44–5, 58, 80
change 48–50, 56–8, 80, 91–2
Christianity 11, 49
communication 34–5
community 44–5, 80–1
consciousness *see* tree of life
courage 28–30, 59–60

creation myth 13–15
creativity 39–41, 63, 67–9, 135

Dagaz (D) 91–2
dark night of the soul 52, 91–2
death 59–60, 74, 81
defense 64–6
desires 27, 41, 43, 51–2
destruction and chaos 48–50
direction, finding 67–9
divination 96–7, 100–1, 104–12
 casting runes 112
 Magic on the Moors 127
 meditations 101–3, 108–9
 questions 100–1, 113, 124
 reading for others 113
 Reading Runes in the Land 124–5
 spreads 104, 105, 106–7, 110, 111
 in the urban landscape 126
 witch walks 121–2, 126, 127
dreams 84
dwarves 15

Ehwaz (E) 77–9
Eihwaz (EI, AE, Y) 59–60
elements 99, 110
elk 65–6
elves 14
emotions 82–4, 110, 137
endings 91–2
equipment 98–9

fate 51, 61–3, 83, 93, 106–8
Fehu (F) 26–7, 133
Fenrir 70
fertility 26–7, 74–9, 85–7
Freyja 14, 24, 26–7, 78, 81, 133
Freyja and Freyr's Ætt 23, 24–45
Freyr 14, 24, 57, 78, 85, 86

galdr 128–30
gaming 61–3
Gebo (G) 42–3
giants 13–15, 28, 31–2
gift-giving 42–3
grounding 101
growth 74–6, 85–7
Gylfaginning 12, 28–9, 41, 42, 72, *140*

Hagalaz (H) 48–50
hamingja 27, 62
hamr 64, *140*
hardship 51
harvest 56–8
Hávamál 12, 16, 34, *140*
hawks 81
healing 28–30, 67–9, 82–4, 131–8
Heimdall 66, 81
Heimdall's Ætt 46–69
Helheim 14, 46
horses 36–7, 75, 77–9

Iðunn 40–1, 62, 81
Inguz (Ng) 85–7
inscriptions 11
intelligence 15, 80–1
introspection 53–5
intuition 113, 137
Isa (I) 53–5

Jera (J) 56–8
jötnar/Jötunheim 14, 32, *140*
journals 99
journeying 16–19, 36–8, 77–9
joy 44–5
justice 72–3

Kenaz (K, C) 39–41
kennings 12, *140*

Laguz (L) 82–4, 137

land spirits 126, 130

life cycle 74–6, 87

life force 26–7, 102, 133

liminal places/beings 65, 83, 86

Loki 75, 81

luck 27, 61–3

Mannaz (M) 80–1

meditations 16–19, 101, 102–3, 108–9, 138

mystery 61–3, 93

Nauthiz (N) 51–2

need and necessity 51–2

Norns 15, 49, 51, 62, 83, 106–9

Odin 13–15, 16–19, 43, 45, 80, 93, 96, 127, 139, *140*

  horse Sleipnir 36–7, 75, 77–8

  Odin's rune 34–5

  and Yggdrasil 16, 34, 111

Othala (O) 88–90

paganism 11, 88, 97, 126

patience 53–5, 93

Perthro (P) 61–3

poems 12, 131

Poetic Edda 12, 16, *140 see also*
  Hávamál; *Völundarkviða*; *Völuspá*

protection 31–3, 59–60, 64–6

querent 113, *140*

Ragnarök 12, 46, *140*

Raidho (R) 36–8

Raven-God *see* Odin

relationships 77–9

renewal 59–60, 74–6

rune bags/boxes 98

rune cloths 99

runes 9, 98, 112 *see also* divination

  creating 116–20

  healing with 131–8

  history of 10–19

  Invoking the Runes 138

  in nature 121–30

  singing the runes 128–30

sacrifice 42–3, 72–3

saga(s) 43, 65, 128, 131, *140*

seiðr 24, 78, 128, *140*

self-love 26–7, 133

sensuality 26–7, 133

Sigrdrífumál 32, 41, 72, 91, 131, *140*

Skáldskaparmál 12, 82, *140*

Skuld 51, 106–7

Sleipnir 36–7, 75, 77–8

Snorri's Edda 12, *140 see also*
  Gylfaginning; *Skáldskaparmál*

sorrow 44–5

Sowilo (S) 67–9, 135

stillness 53–5, 101–3

strength 28–30, 59–60, 134

sun 67–9, 105, 135

swan maidens 64–6

Teiwaz (T) 72–3

Thor 14, 31, 32, 37

thorns 31–3

Thurisaz (Th) 31–3

transformation 39–41, 91–2

tree lore and magic 118–19

tree of life *see* Yggdrasil

trust 77–9

truth 72–3

Týr 70, 72–3, 83

Týr's Ætt 70–93

Urðarbrunnr 15, 62, 65, 83, 107, 108, *140*

Urðr 29, 49, 106–7

Uruz (U) 28–30, 134

Valkyrie(s) 64–6, *140*

Vanir gods 14, 24, *140*

Verðandi 54, 106–7

Völundarkviða 65, *140*

Völuspá 12, *140*

warmth 67–9, 135

water element 29, 82–4

wealth 26–7, 133

Wayland 40

Wild Hunt 49, 74, *140*

wisdom 34–5, 59–60, 83, 89–90, 106–9

witch walks 121–2, 126, 127

wood, working with 117–19

Wunjo (W) 44–5, 80

wyrd 140 see also fate; Urðarbrunnr

yew trees 59

Yggdrasil 15, 16, 34, 59, 66, 83, 107, 111, *140*

Acknowledgments

Thanks to all the CICO publishing team, especially to Carmel Edmonds and Imogen Valler-Miles for all their support and patience with this wonderful project. Thanks to Emma Taylor for her rich and fabulous illustrations.

Lots of love and thanks to my mum for her support and belief, and to my favorite queen and feline companion, Star.

Special thanks to the brilliant Lu Hersey for the runic encouragement, friendship, and reading my drafts; Maggie Rose Cunningham and the Masters of the Runiverse for the deep wisdom-sharing and bright laughter; the wonderful Anna Bemelmans and Vanessa Isobel Black for listening to my runic rambles; the excellent team at the Institute of Northern Studies, in particular Dr Oisín Plumb and Dr Andrew Jennings; and to my UHI Valkyrja, Harley and Jay.

Enormous thanks to my dear friends Jennifer Carr, Esther and Martin Winckles, Jenny Holmes, Trixie Belle Baume, Becky Evans, Kirstie Costar, Annabel Du Boulay, Tiffany Wardle, Anna McKerrow, Sophie and James, Inbaal, Alex Davies, Kay Gillard, Chris Down, Silje Soldal, and to all those, seen and unseen, who have supported me over the years.

Finally, ultimate gratitude to the runes, to the gods, and to all the wild creatures who dwell in this beautiful and sacred land.